Standing Firm

Janet Ruth

ISBN: 978-1-7334184-0-9

DEDICATION

To Andrew and Katie.

Of all the things I would like to teach you,
the words of wisdom in this book
may be the most important.

.

CONTENTS

INTRODUCTION

1-17-24

This book contains two themes. One is learning to understand and use the armor of God referenced in Ephesians 6:10-18; the other is learning to trust God. Those may seem like two very different themes that should be the subject of two different books, but I think you'll see as you go along how well they fit together.

It isn't a long book. You could probably read through it in one sitting or over a quiet weekend, but I would encourage you to go more slowly. When a soldier gets new armor, it takes time to get used to it—one piece at a time—until he or she understands what each piece is about, how to wear it, and how to use it for his or her protection. A new weapon also needs to be broken in and practiced with for many days before the soldier is ready to use it effectively. As you read this book and learn about the armor of God, it is best if you take your time and think about each new thing you read to see how it applies to your life, and then put into practice what you have learned.

This book can be used for personal study or for a group Bible study. Each chapter contains questions to consider or discuss, verses to look up, and suggestions for ways to practice your new skills. Ideally, you should read one chapter each week and then follow the suggestions for that chapter to the best of your ability. You can also find ideas for group activities for each chapter at my website, *www.JaneTruth.com/ StandingFirm*.

If you are a group leader, please read the appendix at the back of this book which talks about how to become a Christian. Be prepared to direct your group there anytime there are questions about what it means to be a Christian.

I hope as you read this book and consider its words, you will learn to stand firm on the promises of God and to live victoriously for him!

1

WAR AND REMEMBRANCE

Many years ago, my daughter created an exhibit for school about the attack on Pearl Harbor during World War II. The historical pictures she used were in black and white. The recording she played of a song from 1945 sounded scratchy and far away. To my twelve-year-old daughter, the events she was studying seemed like ancient history, although they occurred less than a century ago.

I wasn't alive during the attack on Pearl Harbor. But I do remember a morning in September 2001 when I turned on the television to watch the morning news. A special report was on about a tragic event in New York City where a plane had flown, apparently by accident, into one of the buildings of the World Trade Center. As I watched the live report, a second plane flew into the building's twin, exploding into flames and thick clouds of black smoke. No longer did anyone believe the first collision had been an accident. We were under attack, and the heart of New York City was the target.

As the morning unfolded, the target broadened. A third plane hit the Pentagon; then a fourth plane, flying toward Washington, D.C., came down in a field in Pennsylvania. In all, some 3,000 people lost their lives that day in an unexpected and unprovoked attack on United States soil.

In the years since the 9/11 attacks, the United States has been in a continuous war on terror, with the military fighting abroad and government agencies trying to keep ahead of threats at home. Domestic terrorism is on the rise as well, with shootings at schools, malls, and other public places adding to our rising anxiety levels.

We no longer live in a world where our safety and security can be taken for granted, where we can rely on the government to screen out every risk from foreign or domestic enemies, and where the sheer size and power of our nation will provide a wall of protection others fear to breach. In fact, it has never been wise to take our security for granted.

Being aware of potential dangers and prepared to meet them is the only way to deal with the powers of darkness and evil in this world—both the physical world and the spiritual world. In the spiritual world, we have enemies who more than rival our earthly foes; they far surpass them.

The Bible tells us:

> *Be self-controlled and alert. Your enemy the devil prowls around like a roaring lion looking for someone to devour. Resist him,* ***standing firm in the faith****, because you know that your brothers throughout the world are undergoing the same kind of sufferings.* (1 Peter 5:8–9)

In the United States, we grumble about being persecuted if sales clerks refuse to say "Merry Christmas," or our children cannot pray openly at school, or our religious beliefs are mocked by politicians or pop stars. But there are far greater forms of persecution active in the world today. Churches are being burned down, men and women are being put in prison, families are being placed under surveillance, and people are being killed— all because of their witness for Jesus Christ.

Is this right? Is this what God intends for his children? Or is there some way to prevent these things, to hold off our enemies, and to live in peace? Didn't Jesus promise we would have peace? So why do we have to deal with war, persecution, and uncertainty? Why do Christians throughout the world have to live with a constant threat of violence and loss, and why does it seem that just being a Christian puts a target on your back for ridicule, dismissal, and even violence?

These are hard questions, but God has answers. We must look to God's Word if we are to understand what is happening in our world and how God wants us to respond.

> ❓ Do you believe we are safer in our country than we were
> two decades ago or less safe? Why do you think that is?

From Here to Eternity

Many people are familiar with these words of Isaiah prophesying a time when all the people of the world will live in peace:

> *They will beat their swords into plowshares and their spears into pruning hooks. Nation will not take up sword against nation, nor will they train for war anymore.* (Isaiah 2:4b)

We long for those days and wish they would come in our lifetime. Then we could settle down in this world God created for us and live without fear or distress. The problem is that the Bible talks about a whole course of events which must take place before that great day arrives, and we must understand where we are in those events.

When Jesus spoke of the future, he didn't use the same inspiring words Isaiah did. Asked by his disciples, *"When will this happen, and what will be the sign of your coming and of the end of the age?"* Jesus answered:

> *Watch out that no one deceives you. For many will come in my name, claiming, "I am the Christ," and will deceive many. You will hear of wars and rumors of wars, but see to it that you are not alarmed. Such things must happen, but the end is still to come. Nation will rise against nation, and kingdom against kingdom. There will be famines and earthquakes in various places. All these are the beginning of birth pains.*

Then you will be handed over to be persecuted and put to death, and you will be hated by all nations because of me. At that time many will turn away from the faith and will betray and hate each other, and many false prophets will appear and deceive many people. Because of the increase of wickedness, the love of most will grow cold, but he who **stands firm** *to the end will be saved. And this gospel of the kingdom will be preached in the whole world as a testimony to all nations, and then the end will come.* (Matthew 24:4–14)

So when do the *good* times come?

The last book of the Bible, Revelation, picks up the story after the dark days Jesus predicted. There will be a great battle between good and evil that ends with Satan being tied up and thrown into a lake of fire. Then Jesus will reign as king over all the earth for a thousand years (Revelation 19:11–20:6). After the thousand years, there will be *"a new heaven and a new earth"* (21:1), and God's people will live in his presence in the New Jerusalem, a city of *"pure gold, as pure as glass"* (21:18). *"He will wipe every tear from their eyes. There will be no more death or mourning or crying or pain, for the old order of things has passed away"* (21:4).

Those are the good times waiting for us. That's our future—a beautiful city, a perfect world, where the tree of life grows, and where it is said, *"no longer will there be any curse"* (Revelation 22:3).

Where are we now?

We're in an imperfect world, kicked out of Eden, living under a curse that touches every part of our lives.

Where did that curse come from?

To answer that, we must take our eyes away from the end of time and look back to the beginning. There we find Adam and Eve living in the Garden of Eden, a beautiful, peaceful place made by God for the use of the people he created. Satan, in the form of a serpent, tempted Eve to eat the fruit of a tree God said not to eat. Eve ate the fruit. Adam ate the fruit. When God asked what they had done, Adam blamed Eve and Eve blamed the serpent. God punished them all by removing them from the Garden of Eden and placing them under a curse (Genesis 3:1–24).

> ➢ God cursed the ground, the very earth he had created for his people (Genesis 3:17–18).

> ➢ He cursed the relationship between Adam and Eve and through them all of humanity (3:16).

> ➢ He laid a curse on Satan, making him forever the enemy of mankind, just as Satan had already made himself the enemy of God (3:15).

> ➢ Finally, God had warned Adam and Eve if they ate fruit from the forbidden tree they would *"surely die"* (2:17). Because of their disobedience, their bodies would one day cease to function and would return to the dust of the ground from which they were taken (3:19).

It turned out, though, that the curse of death held a hidden blessing: an end to life on this cursed and blemished earth and an opportunity to walk with God again, unhindered by sin and temptation, unbothered by threats of wars or persecution, eternally at peace, and no longer standing guard against the forces of evil.

You see, it helps to know where we came from, and it helps to know where we're going. **Right now, we're in the middle of the story where conflict abounds and all is frightening and uncertain—except to those who have read to the end of the book.**

For now, our job is to stand firm and remain on guard against the enemies of God. But our blessed future isn't so far away, and God's promise is sure.

He who stands firm to the end will be saved.

Matthew 24:13

A Final Word

This chapter may have been uncomfortable for some of you. Perhaps you haven't been a Christian for long. Or perhaps you've never been taught about spiritual warfare, persecution, and the end times. You may be thinking, "This isn't what I signed on for when I became a Christian."

It's easy as a believer to look for the encouraging parts of the Bible—the verses that tell us God loves us and will provide for our needs. We like to think God will make everything better for us because he is our loving Father. We blame the violence and hatred in our world on other people, thinking if we could just get them to behave better everything would be all right. But if we read the Bible literally, especially the warnings about persecution and the end times, we need to accept the fact that things are not going to get better. Not really. Never for long.

We live in a cursed world, and we have a spiritual enemy determined to do us harm. We must learn what God has to say about defending ourselves and fighting the battles that are ours to fight!

The following chapters will talk about who our enemy is and how God equips us with his "armor" to stand firm against the enemy's schemes. Most of all, this is a book about learning to trust God. The Bible tells us much about the world, how it will end, and what comes after, but it doesn't reveal all God's secrets. **Like a good author, he's holding back some surprises to keep us guessing and, most importantly, to keep us trusting him.**

Consider:

What do you believe the Bible says about the future of our world? Are the "end times" something you are looking forward to, or something you dread? Why?

Do you think Jesus was talking about *you* when he said, "You will be hated by all nations because of me" (Matthew 24:9)? What about when he said, "If they persecuted me, they will persecute you also" (John 15:20)?

What do you think of Paul's warning, "Everyone who wants to live a godly life in Christ Jesus will be persecuted" (2 Timothy 3:12)?

Look up:

Look up and think about the following verses that help us understand the purpose of suffering. Write them out below and consider underlining them in your Bible to help you remember them.

Romans 5:1-5: _Faith, hope & love p 1700_
Expect Endurance

James 1:2-4: 1870 _faith produces perseverance_

Romans 8:35 and 37-39: 1703 /

Will anguish or distress or persecutions
or famine or nakedness or peril or the
sword

We conquer through Him

Apply:

It's easy to dismiss things happening in far off lands as unimportant to us, but we must remember that the suffering of fellow Christians, wherever they are, is the suffering of our brothers and sisters in Christ.

Take a look at *The Voice of the Martyrs* website (www.persecution.com). Find one person or group on the website you can pray for this week. Write out their name here:

_____

Read Chapter 2 → 7   See 7ᵗʰ my house

2

GETTING READY

One of my favorite books of the Bible is Nehemiah in the Old Testament. Nehemiah lived during a time when the nation of Israel had been defeated by the Babylonian Empire and many of its people sent away to live in exile. After many long years, the people were allowed to return to their homeland and rebuild their cities. When Nehemiah arrived in Jerusalem, he found it in a sorry state, with most of the city wall broken down and the gates burned.

Until modern times, towns and cities had to have walls, ditches, or other fortifications to protect their inhabitants from attack by foreign armies, raiding bandits, and wild animals. Victorious armies would tear down the walls of conquered cities to keep the people there from defending themselves in the future.

Although Israel was still under the control of a foreign nation when the Jews began to return, Nehemiah came with permission to rebuild Jerusalem's wall. Not everyone liked the idea though. When Nehemiah got the work started, others living in the land threatened to attack the Jews to get them to stop. But Nehemiah made a plan and encouraged the people:

"We'll post guards all night, and during the day everyone will work with a sword at their side. Half of the people will stand guard with spears while the other half work. If everyone does their share, we can get this job done!" (Nehemiah 4:16–23, paraphrased).

They did get the job done. In 52 days, the wall around the city and all the gates were built or repaired. Such a feat would be considered amazing even in today's advanced societies. In 445 B.C., it was nothing less than miraculous. Nehemiah knew who deserved the credit. He wrote:

When all our enemies heard about this, all the surrounding nations were afraid and lost their self-confidence, because they realized that this work had been done with the help of our God. (Nehemiah 6:16)

Before they had a wall of protection around them, the Jews had been forced to compromise with the surrounding nations and do things their way. The neighboring countries liked having power over the Jews, and they were willing to fight to keep that power. Nehemiah encouraged his people to pick up their weapons and be prepared to fight back. That was the only way they would ever be able to have a secure place to live.

Nehemiah had a lot of important things going for him. He understood his enemies and what they were capable of doing. He understood what God wanted him to do. He created a detailed plan, and he encouraged his people to follow it. Most of all, he trusted God and in the promise God made to restore his chosen people to the land of Israel.

When the Jews had been defeated and taken away into exile, God had spoken to them through the prophet Jeremiah:

This is what the Lord says: "When seventy years are completed for Babylon, I will come to you and fulfill my gracious promise to bring you back to this place.

"For I know the plans I have for you," declares the Lord, "plans to prosper you and not to harm you, plans to give you hope and a future. *Then you will call upon me and come and pray to me, and I will listen to you. You will seek me and find me when you seek me with all your heart."* (Jeremiah 29:10–13)

Just like the people of Nehemiah's day, we need to be ready to stand up to our enemy. To do that, we need to understand who our enemy is and what he's up to. We need to know how to fight our battles and defend ourselves. And we need to remember that God will lead us to victory. **Without that assurance we might as well give up—we've already been defeated.**

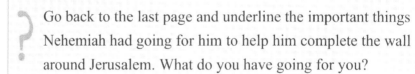

? Go back to the last page and underline the important things Nehemiah had going for him to help him complete the wall around Jerusalem. What do you have going for you?

Our Enemy

So who is our enemy? On a national level, you might think of terrorists, foreign armies, or members of whichever political party you don't belong to. If you're thinking about enemies of God's people, you might identify atheists, evolutionists, and the liberal court system. But none of these is the enemy we're talking about here.

The apostle Paul wrote,

> *For our struggle is not against flesh and blood, but against the rulers, against the authorities, against the powers of this dark world and against the spiritual forces of evil in the heavenly realms.* (Ephesians 6:12)

In the verse just before this, he wrote,

> *Put on the full armor of God so that you can take your stand against the devil's schemes.* (Ephesians 6:11)

Yes, our enemy is the devil.

His name is Satan, which is the Greek word for a false witness or a slanderer. The Bible calls him (SATIN)

the evil one – Matthew 13:38

a murderer – John 8:44

the father of lies – John 8:44

15

SATIN is *the prince of this world* – John 12:31, 14:30

the god of this age – 2 Corinthians 4:4

the ruler of the kingdom of the air - Ephesians 2:2

That means we're not only engaged in a spiritual battle—we're fighting behind enemy lines!

What else do we know about Satan? The Bible never gives us a complete description of him or his origins, but we're given many glimpses of him doing battle against God's people.

- ➢ In the first book of the Bible, we meet Satan in the Garden of Eden tempting the first man and woman to disobey God's command (Genesis 3:1–6).

- ➢ We find him again in the book of Job making accusations and bringing disaster on an obedient man to goad him into rejecting God (Job 1:6–11).

- ➢ He *"rose up against Israel"* and tempted King David to make a terrible mistake (1 Chronicles 21:1).

- ➢ He *"snatches away"* the meaning of the gospel from the hearts of the unsaved and blinds their minds to the truth (Matthew 13:19; 2 Corinthians 4:4).

- ➢ He interferes with the work of God's people and is out to destroy them (1 Thessalonians 2:18; 1 Peter 5:8).

16

Even Jesus was directly tempted by Satan (Matthew 4:1–11). So, don't think you're going to get off easy!

Satan isn't a myth, and he isn't a metaphor for all that is evil in our world. He is real. Like God, he is a spiritual being, not made of flesh and blood like we are. But unlike God, there are limits to his power and his authority (Job 1:6–12, 2:1–7; 2 Thessalonians 2:7–8). He could not stop Jesus from living a sinless life or rising from the dead, and he can't change the sentence that has been pronounced against him and he will one day have to serve (Revelation 20:10).

For now, he has great authority on the earth and a mission to disrupt God's plans to the best of his abilities. But God has not left us defenseless!

In the rest of this book, we'll talk about some of the specific ways Satan attacks and how we can be prepared to defend ourselves against him. We have to remember, though, that we cannot destroy Satan or defeat him. He has his part to play until Jesus returns to earth for the final battle. In relation to Satan, we have only one mission:

STAND FIRM!

The Bible tells us:

> *No temptation has seized you except what is common to man. And God is faithful; he will not let you be tempted beyond what you can bear. But when you are tempted, he will also provide a way out so that you can **stand up** under it.* (1 Corinthians 10:13)

> *Be self-controlled and alert. Your enemy the devil prowls around like a roaring lion looking for someone to devour. Resist him, **standing firm** in the faith, because you know that your brothers throughout the world are undergoing the same kind of sufferings.* (1 Peter 5:8–9)

> *Be patient, then, brothers, until the Lord's coming. See how the farmer waits for the land to yield its valuable crop and how patient he is for the autumn and spring rains. You too, be patient and **stand firm**, because the Lord's coming is near.* (James 5:7–8)

And, in the words of Jesus:

> *Brother will betray brother to death, and a father his child. Children will rebel against their parents and have them put to death. All men will hate you because of me, but he who **stands firm** to the end will be saved.* (Mark 13:12–13)

> What do you think it means to *stand firm*? Do you think it's an easy thing or a hard thing to do?

Our Hope

Stand firm. That's the goal. Although there are many things which can help us stand firm, the most important is the hope we have when we trust in God. Just like God had plans for the Jews of the fifth century BC, he has plans for you, too, and he has the power to help you succeed in those plans.

As long as you remember his promises and put your trust in him, he will give you the strength to stand firm against Satan's attacks. Satan wants to turn your attention away from God, to get you to let your guard down, to separate you from the one who has promised to take care of you. **If you want to win this battle, you've got to keep your heart and mind focused on God.**

Peter, one of Jesus' closest friends during his life on earth, summed up our hope in Christ this way:

> *Praise be to the God and Father of our Lord Jesus Christ! In his great mercy he has given us new birth into a living hope through the resurrection of Jesus Christ from the dead, and into an inheritance that can never perish, spoil or fade—kept in heaven for you, who through faith are shielded by God's power until the coming of the salvation that is ready to be revealed in the last time. In this you greatly rejoice, though now for a little while you may have had to suffer grief in all kinds of trials. These have come so that your faith—of greater worth than gold, which perishes even though refined by fire—may be proved genuine and may result in praise, glory and honor when Jesus Christ is revealed. Though you*

have not seen him, you love him; and even though you do not see him now, you believe in him and are filled with an inexpressible and glorious joy, for you are receiving the goal of your faith, the salvation of your souls.

Therefore, prepare your minds for action; be self–controlled; set your hope fully on the grace to be given you when Jesus Christ is revealed. (1 Peter 1:3–9, 13)

What did Peter say we could put our hope in?

- ➤ **An inheritance that can never perish, spoil or fade**
- ➤ **Faith—of greater worth than gold**
- ➤ **Praise, glory, and honor**
- ➤ **An inexpressible and glorious joy, and**
- ➤ **The goal of your faith, the salvation of your souls.**

Those are excellent promises, and they are available to anyone who believes in Jesus and has turned to him for salvation. The Bible is filled with promises and reminders that God loves you and he wants the best for you. Claiming these promises as your own is the first step to building up your defense against your enemy, the devil. Your job is to remember those promises and to take courage from them!

Our Battle

When you became a Christian by accepting Jesus Christ as your Savior, you became a child of God. You also switched sides in the great battle between Satan and God.

Once you were alienated from God and were enemies in your minds because of your evil behavior. But now he has reconciled you by Christ's physical body through death to present you holy in his sight, without blemish and free from accusation. (Colossians 1:21–22)

Satan's great hatred toward God now extends to you as well, and he would like nothing better than to stop you from being an effective soldier in God's army (Luke 22:31). That makes each one of us a target for his evil schemes (Ephesians 6:11–12). The objective of our enemy is two-fold: to keep us from enjoying our relationship with God and to keep us from living lives that bring glory to God.

Just like the Jews of Nehemiah's day had to work hard to build up their defenses, we also have to defend the things God has promised us.

Peace with God, protection from temptation, contentment and joy, hope for the future—these are all things Satan would like to take away from us. If he can get us to stop relying on God to provide these things, he wins the battle! But we have God's promise that if we do our part we can beat Satan.

> For everyone born of God overcomes the world. This is the victory that has overcome the world, even our faith. Who is it that overcomes the world? Only he who believes that Jesus is the Son of God. (1 John 5:4–5)

A Final Word

So, how is your battle going?

Have your spiritual defenses broken down over time as you turned your mind to other things? Have you dropped your guard against the enemy because you're too tired, or too busy, or you just haven't thought about it lately? Do you find it easier to appease your enemy—the devil—by going along with the ways of the world instead of working hard to maintain a defense? Or perhaps you didn't know you needed a defense. Maybe fighting spiritual battles is a new concept to you, and you need to learn how to start building up a defense.

This book is a good place to start. The Bible is the best place, and we'll spend a lot of time looking at God's Word while we work through building up a solid defense against Satan's attacks. Let the Word of God be your wall of protection against the attacks of our enemy, the devil, and let God's promises of hope be the foundation of your defense.

The psalmist said:

> *The Lord is my rock, my fortress and my deliverer; my God is my rock, in whom I take refuge. He is my shield and the horn of my salvation, my stronghold. I call to the Lord, who is worthy of praise, and I am saved from my enemies.* (Psalm 18:2–3)

Consider:

What are you doing to remember God's promises of hope? Reading the Bible regularly helps us remember God's promises and rely on them.

Another great way to think about God's promises is to listen to Christian music during the week. Are there any Christian radio stations where you live? Can you put Christian CD's in your car or add gospel songs to your playlists? If you are in a group study, share with each other your favorite types of Christian music or your favorite Christian artists.

Look up:

Look up the following verses about hope and write them out here.

2 Corinthians 3:12 _Since we have such a hope we are bold_

Ephesians 1:18: _The eyes and the hunt open_

2 Thessalonians 2:16–17: _may our lord JC himself and by the father give Encourage and strengthen you in every thought and deed_

1 Timothy 6:17: _____

Command the wealthy not to put their wealth in money but strength in Gods

Apply:

Reading God's Word and listening to Christian music are excellent ways to keep our thoughts focused on God and his promises, but we can do more than that. Begin this week to surround yourself with reminders of the hope we have in Christ Jesus.

Look up some encouraging verses and write or print them out. Put one on the refrigerator, a couple in your desk at work or a school binder. Look at them often and try to commit them to memory. If you are artistic, draw or paint scenes that include encouraging words from the Bible.

If you are in a group study, create something you can copy and share with members of your group and bring it to your next meeting!

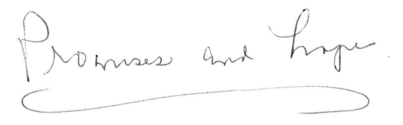

3

THE BELT OF TRUTH

Have you ever played dodge ball? You know the game: you take a ball and throw it at your opponents. If you hit them, they're out; if they catch the ball, you're out. There are several ways to play the game—in a circle, on two sides, with or without a "jail."

Some people love the game. They grab as many balls as they can, throw them as hard as they can, and beg to get back into the game whenever they're tagged out. Others hate the game. They never pick up a ball and spend all their time trying to avoid being hit. Or worse, they make sure they get hit right at the beginning of the game and then sit peacefully at the sidelines ignoring the battle raging in front of them and doing nothing to help their team.

The spiritual war we fight against Satan is like dodge ball, only it's a lot more serious.

Once we have joined the army of God, we are on his team for good. Satan can't pull us onto his side, but he can attack us. He can tag us out for a while.

He can even discourage us enough that we take ourselves out of the game and sit on the sidelines ignoring the war all around us. When we're fighting in our own strength, without training and without the right defenses, we can spend a lot of time being "out" instead of in the battle putting up a good fight. But there is no reason why you can't be a topnotch soldier in God's army. God is ready and willing to help you every step of the way.

The apostle Paul gave a great description of Christian life as a battleground between God and Satan:

> *Finally, be strong in the Lord and in his mighty power. Put on the full* **armor of God** *so that you can take your stand against the devil's schemes. For our struggle is not against flesh and blood, but against the rulers, against the authorities, against the powers of this dark world and against the spiritual forces of evil in the heavenly realms.* (Ephesians 6:10–12)

If you read the words carefully, it sounds pretty scary. But in the sentences that follow, Paul tells us how to be ready to stand firm against the enemy's attacks:

> *Therefore put on the full* **armor of God**, *so that when the day of evil comes, you may be able to stand your ground, and after you have done everything, to stand.* **Stand firm** *then, with the belt of truth buckled around your waist, with the breastplate of righteousness in place, and with your feet fitted with the readiness that comes from the gospel of peace. In addition to all this, take up the shield of faith, with which you can extinguish all the flaming*

arrows of the evil one. Take the helmet of salvation and the sword of the Spirit, which is the Word of God. And pray in the Spirit on all occasions with all kinds of prayers and requests. With this in mind, be alert and always keep on praying for all the saints. (Ephesians 6:13–18)

When Paul wrote this letter, he was writing to people in the same boat we are in. What they needed was armor that would allow them to stand up under Satan's continuing attacks and let them be both **safe** and **victorious** in their spiritual battles. Paul told his fellow Christians about seven things that would provide all the protection they would ever need. The first item is the Belt of Truth.

What is Truth?

When Jesus was on the earth, teaching and preaching about the Kingdom of God, people didn't always understand him. He spoke in parables and said things which didn't make sense to his Jewish audience. A lot of people questioned him, some out of a sincere desire to understand and others out of a malicious desire to trap him into saying something wrong.

In the Gospel of John, written by one of Jesus' closest followers, we see an amazing pronouncement:

*To the Jews who had believed him, Jesus said, "if you hold to my teaching, you are really my disciples. Then you will know the truth, and **the truth will set you free**"* (John 8:31–32).

Not long after this, Jesus stood before a Roman governor accused by the Jewish leaders of claiming to be the Son of God and King of the Jews. Jesus admitted to Pilate that he was a king, although not a king of this world.

"You are a king, then!" said Pilate.

Jesus answered, "You are right in saying I am a king. In fact, for this reason I was born, and for this I came into the world, to testify to the truth. ***Everyone on the side of truth listens to me.****"*

"What is truth?" Pilate asked. (John 18:37–39)

What is Truth?

It's a tough question, especially in today's world. We are constantly challenged to keep an open mind. We are told to not be judgmental. In the battle of ideas, we are asked to find a way to compromise. I'm sure you've heard this one: "There are so many different beliefs about God and salvation. It's very closed-minded to believe that only one is right and all the others are wrong."

When you hear these kinds of statements, ask yourself this: is this Jesus talking or the enemy?

About himself, Jesus said, *"I am the way and the truth and the life. No one comes to the Father except through me"* (John 14:6). But about Satan, Jesus said, *"He was a murderer from the beginning, not holding to the truth, for there is no truth in him. When he lies, he speaks his native language, for he is a liar and the father of lies"* (John 8:44).

Satan is a liar!

Remembering that is the first piece of armor you need to defend yourself from Satan's attacks. Jesus, on the other hand, never lied!

I did a word search of the New Testament, and I was amazed how many times Jesus said, *"I tell you the truth."* It's in all four gospels again and again. *"I tell you the truth."* He wanted to impress it on our hearts and minds.

What Jesus has to say is TRUE!

We can believe it, and we can stand firm in that belief.

In the Gospel of John, Jesus is described as the one *"who came from the Father, full of grace and truth"* (John 1:14). The Holy Spirit is described as the *"Spirit of truth ... [who] will guide you into all truth"* (John 16:13). And when Jesus prayed for his disciples, he asked God to *"sanctify them by the truth; [for] your word is truth"* (John 17:17). To "sanctify" something is to set it apart as something special. Jesus prayed that God would make us—his disciples, his soldiers—sanctified, or set apart, by the truth.

The first essential piece of armor is the belt of **TRUTH**. Believe that there is truth. Know that God is the author of that truth, that Jesus always spoke the truth, and that the Word of God, the Bible, is true. Although you will never in your life know all the truth of God or understand everything about God or his Word, you can be sure God does know, and he will equip you with the truth you need to stand firm.

> ? In the last paragraph, underline the four great truths we should remember. Do you struggle with any of these?

Satan's Weapons of Mass Destruction

Satan lies.

Although that may not sound like a battle strategy, Satan's greatest weapons are lies.

If he can get people to believe there is no God, they will not honor him as they should and turn to him for salvation. If he can convince people God will not judge or punish them, they feel free to live lives that are opposed to God's law. If he can fool people into believing they are good and capable, they will not cling to God. If he can get them to believe they are worthless, they will not call out to God. If he can get them to believe there is time, they will put God off.

Satan has many lies which he directs against us as individuals, and we will talk about those more in the chapter on faith. Right now, let's look at the lies Satan is using as his weapons of mass destruction.

Lie Number One: There is no God.

This one isn't new. Long before Jesus lived on the earth, his forefather David said, *"The fool says in his heart 'there is no God'"* (Psalm 14:1). Today, many people look to science to explain the wonders of the universe and the incredible workings of the human mind and spirit. Magazines, TV shows, and even school textbooks declare that we have the cosmos all figured out and there is no reason to believe in a creator God.

The Bible, on the other hand, says:

For since the creation of the world, God's invisible qualities—his eternal power and divine nature—have been clearly seen, being understood from what has been made, so that men are without excuse. (Romans 1:20)

No Love,
No punishment

If you are a Christian, you have already reached the conclusion that there is a God. But even Christians face times of doubt when everything you thought you knew about God seems unconvincing and empty. It's in those times you must listen again to the voice of Jesus and do your best to tune out the lies of the enemy. Read your Bible, pray for wisdom, and don't let yourself be a casualty to Lie Number One.

Lie Number Two: There are many Gods, or one God of many natures.

One of the leading philosophies of our day is that "all paths lead to heaven." People want to believe that if they are good, if they believe in God or destiny or spirituality, and if they are true to themselves and their own belief system, they will find God—or nirvana—or peace—or fulfillment in the afterlife. This way, everyone is comfortable, we are each the judge of our own behavior, and we can live in peace with one another.

It is true that after life, everyone will find God, but many people will not find him as they want him to be. In the Book of Revelation we see that day:

Then I saw a great white throne and him who was seated on it. Earth and sky fled from his presence, and there was no place for them. And I saw the dead, great and small, standing before the throne, and books were opened. Another book was opened, which is the book of life. The dead were judged according to what they had done as recorded in the books ... If anyone's name was not found written in the book of life, he was thrown into the lake of fire. (Revelation 20:11–12, 15)

There is one God, and there is one path to heaven. Anyone who believes otherwise will find himself spending eternity in a lake of fire. Don't let Satan fool you with Lie Number Two.

Lie Number Three: The Bible is not true.

If someone has fallen for either of the first two lies, they believe this one as well. Many people, though, believe in God and believe in heaven and hell, but do not believe in the absolute authority of the Bible. Others turn away from God because they lose faith in the Bible. The reliability of the Bible is certainly under attack these days, and those attacks are all being planned and directed by that great liar, Satan.

We are told there is "evidence" that Jesus didn't die on the cross and that he wasn't the Son of God. We hear that the early church fathers concocted stories and suppressed the truth about Jesus. Some claim the Jews made up much of the history we find in the Old Testament, so that isn't reliable either. And many Christians will tell you that parts of the Bible are symbolic only and not meant to be taken literally—like the six days of creation and the final destruction of heaven and earth.

How do you respond to these lies?

By being firmly grounded in the TRUTH!

Attacks against the teachings of Jesus and the apostles aren't new. They started as a direct response to those teachings two thousand years ago. The New Testament is filled with warnings about false teachers who wanted to turn the first believers away from the truth. Paul wrote about them (2 Corinthians 11:13; Galatians 2:4; 1 Timothy 1:3-4). Peter warned against them (2 Peter 2:1). John talked about them (1 John 4:1). Even Jesus told us they would come (Matthew 7:15). In fact, Jesus said the appearance of many false prophets would be one of the signs of the end times before his return to earth (Matthew 24:11). Our answer to these false teachers and prophets is to hold fast to the truth of God, his Son Jesus, and the authority of the Bible. That's a lot better than listening to Lie Number Three.

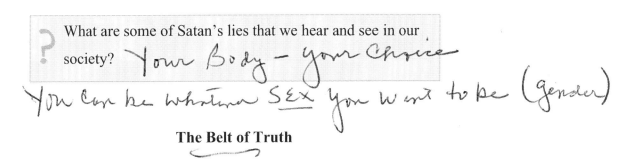

? What are some of Satan's lies that we hear and see in our society? *Your Body – your Choice*

You can be whatever SEX you want to be (gender)

The Belt of Truth

God doesn't want us to go into battle against Satan's lies unprepared and undefended. The first part of battle armor we need is the Belt of Truth. The wide, heavy belt of a Roman soldier kept his tunic in place instead of down around his knees tripping him up, and it protected his abdomen from stabs and blows. The abdomen is a vulnerable part of the body, a place where we can bleed to death even from a shallow wound.

We need to have the truth of God wrapped around us to keep Satan from tripping us up or inflicting a wound which will greatly injure our relationship with God.

Of course, there was another important purpose for the Roman soldier's belt—it held a weapon. Our Belt of Truth also holds a weapon: *the "sword of the Spirit, which is the Word of God"*—the Bible (Ephesians 6:17).

A soldier wouldn't go into battle tired from carrying his sword in his hand all day. That's why he had a belt to carry it on. If we do not trust completely in the truth of God's Word, we will quickly lose our ability to wield it as a sword. If we doubt the Bible's authenticity or try to pick and choose the reliable parts from the unreliable, we will soon tire of trying to figure out what we can believe and what we can't. We'll either drop our sword completely, as many do, or put so many nicks and notches in it that it can't do us any good. Either way, Satan wins.

Luckily, you're not in this battle alone.

There are many excellent books available about the Bible that will help you understand how it was written and put together and why it is truly authentic and reliable. There are also books that explore the teachings of the Bible and explain how they go together and create a powerful argument for the existence of God and his plan of salvation. Ask your pastor or ministry leader to recommend one.

Most importantly, you can prepare yourself by reading your own copy of the Bible and discovering the truth about God and Jesus from their own words. If it seems too difficult to understand at first, remember that the study of the Bible is a lifelong pursuit. God will always have new things to reveal to us in his Word. And, as the Bible says,

> **If any of you lacks wisdom, he should ask God,**
>
> **who gives generously to all without finding fault,**
>
> **and it will be given to him.**
>
> **James 1:5**

I would also urge you to be very cautious about disregarding any part of the Bible, calling it symbolic or a metaphor or no longer true in today's world. As you read the Bible there may be things which seem inconsistent, unimportant, or even impossible. They aren't.

This is the Word of God, the creator and sustainer of the universe, the all-powerful and all-knowing, the one who wrote the pages of time before any of them came to be. This is his personal, loving, purposeful communication with each of us. Don't treat any of it with disdain.

The more you read God's Word and learn about God's Word, the more you will come to trust in the truth of God's Word. And there's no better defense against Satan's lies than that.

Take a moment to look up and write out 2 Timothy 2:15:

PRAY for Discernment

A Final Word

While you're reading books and listening to preachers and teachers and trying to understand the truth about God and his plan for your life, you're going to hear and read things which are *not* true. I would love to tell you that every book you buy in a Christian bookstore and every sermon you hear from a Christian preacher is true. Unfortunately, not all of them are.

Too many people start out relying on the truth but later fall under the spell of Satan's lies. Like spies of the enemy, they live among us and look and talk like us, but their real purpose is to harm our relationship with God. Only by reading and studying the Bible for yourself and praying regularly about what you read can you test the truthfulness of what you hear and read elsewhere.

Relying on the truth of God's Word, and using it as the standard of truth against which all other teachings are tested, will allow you to stand before God as one approved, a workman unashamed, and a soldier ready to do battle for God and his kingdom.

Consider:

How secure is your belt of truth? Are you confused about the claims that Jesus didn't die on the cross? Do you need to know more about how the Bible was written and put together? Do you want to know more about the debate between evolutionists and creationists? If Satan's lies have been coming at you like big, red dodge balls, trying to take you out of the game, don't give up! Talk to your pastor and Bible study teachers. Keep reading your Bible. And find a few reliable books to help you find answers to your questions.

If you are in a group study, make a list of things you have heard about God, Jesus, or the Bible which trouble you. Don't try to analyze them now; just list them. Then consider planning a future Bible study or two around finding the truth about these troubling claims.

Look up:

Write out and compare the following two verses.

John 14:6: _____

_____

_____

John 8:44: _____

_____

_____

_____

Find two verses in the New Testament that include the words "stand firm" or "standing firm" and write them out here:

_____

_____

_____

_____

_____

_____

_____

Apply:

Visit your church library and make a list of books that would help you have a better understanding of the Bible. Remember these books when you face a particular argument against the Bible or against Christianity you don't have an answer for. If there are no books available on topics of interest to you, do some research and ask your church to buy specific books which would be helpful. Perhaps you even have some helpful books at home you can donate to your church library or share with your group members.

Remember, though, not all "Christian" books tell the truth about God and the Bible. Read carefully, and ask your pastor or Bible study leaders about anything that seems confusing or contrary to God's Word.

4

THE BREASTPLATE OF RIGHTEOUSNESS

I have a friend who believes her chances of getting into heaven depend on the kind of life she lives. She sees salvation like a spiritual tightrope. You go through life carrying all the good and evil deeds you have done, and at the end of your life you fall to one side of the tightrope or the other. If you are weighed down by selfishness and evil deeds you fall to eternal punishment. If you are carrying enough good deeds you fall to eternal reward.

Most world religions teach the necessity of good deeds. Hindus believe they will obtain the height of existence through good works, devotion, and meditation. Buddhists believe that "nirvana" is achieved by practicing strict self-discipline. Muslims believe they must obey all the laws of the Qur'an and perform more good deeds than bad. Even the Catholic Church teaches that a person must do good and avoid evil to be saved.

Of course, not everyone believes in the necessity of good works. Some people look in the Bible and read that salvation is gained by faith in Jesus Christ and not by works. Say a prayer, confess your sins, and you're good to go. Heaven is assured, so why worry about the way you live here on earth. Good works can't buy salvation, so they don't really have any purpose, right?

The Bible tells us:

For it is by grace you have been saved, through faith—and this not from yourselves, it is the gift of God—not by works, so that no one can boast. (Ephesians 2:8–9)

But because of his great love for us, God, who is rich in mercy, made us alive with Christ even when we were dead in transgressions—it is by grace you have been saved. (Ephesians 2:4–5)

But the Bible also says:

Faith without works is dead. (James 2:26)

Here we see two more of Satan's lies. One is that we have to do good things to earn God's favor, the other is that it doesn't matter if we do sinful things because we're already saved. The real story lies somewhere in the middle.

The truth is that God does have expectations for your life. He wants you to live a righteous life, a godly life, a life pleasing to him. You don't do this to get into God's family, but because you are already in God's family. You are a child of the King, and you are expected to act like it.

Believe it or not, God wants us to be righteous for our own sake. In fact, the second piece of protection Paul tells us to put on is the breastplate of righteousness. Although it is Jesus' righteousness that covers our sin and makes us right with God, it is our own righteousness—our obedience to God—which enables us to live the kind of life God wants for us and to stand firm against the attacks of the enemy.

> **?** Have you ever worried about not being good enough to get into heaven? What do the verses from Ephesians above say about that?

We get to heaven by GRACE

What is Righteousness?

Righteousness simply means being righteous. The Merriam–Webster dictionary defines "righteous" as "acting or being in accordance with what is just, honorable, and free from guilt or wrong."

Most people think of righteousness as living by a certain code of conduct, doing the things God wants us to do and not doing the things he doesn't want us to do. The Bible has a lot to say about good behavior and bad behavior. You are probably familiar with the Ten Commandments found in Exodus 20 and with Jesus' command to *"do to others what you would have them do to you"* (Matthew 7:12).

But righteousness is about more than what we do or don't do. Paul said, *"If I give all I possess to the poor and surrender my body to the flames, but have not love, I gain nothing"* (1 Corinthians 13:3).

When we love God and we love others, we do good things for them without even thinking about a list of "do's" and "don'ts." Paul prayed for God's people: *"that your love will abound more and more in knowledge and depth of insight, so that you may be able to discern what is best and may be pure and blameless until the day of Christ, filled with the fruit of righteousness that comes through Jesus Christ—to the glory and praise of God"* (Philippians 1:9-11).

In other words, righteousness is a natural outgrowth of loving God and wanting to please him.

Any kind of good works apart from God's love is useless.

Satan's Big Guns

Satan doesn't want you to be righteous. He doesn't want you to do good, or, if you're going to do good, he wants you to do it for the wrong reasons.

Satan has a whole arsenal of weapons to keep you from living the way God wants you to live. He'll try to convince you it doesn't matter if you sin. He'll tell you what you want to do isn't sin. He'll argue you can have a lot more fun, a lot more freedom, a lot more money, a lot more pleasure if you do sin. He's going to do anything he can to convince you to follow his way—which he convincingly passes off as being your way—instead of following God. And, sadly, he's very good at what he does. We all fall for his lies sometimes.

Satan uses many things to keep us off the right path, but they can be put into two groups. They are his big guns, his weapons of choice to destroy our effectiveness as soldiers in God's army.

The first big gun is **temptation**.

It comes in so many forms, it's impossible to discuss them in one book. We are tempted by food, physical pleasure, money, possessions, and a whole host of imagined "needs." The basic lie behind all of these temptations is that what we can get by disobeying God is better than what God promises if we obey him.

The second big gun is **conformity**.

It's hard enough to make the right choices when it only affects you. When everyone around you is making wrong choices, it gets a lot harder, because being different will affect the way other people see you and act toward you. Satan wants you to believe that what you can get from other people— friendship, acceptance, opportunities to do things, and just being liked—is better than what God promises.

FALSE Sense of Right & wrong

> **?** Do you think you have more trouble battling temptation (doing what pleases you) or conformity (doing what pleases others)?

Try to please God. Am not into worldly garbage. Hollywood STINKS —

The music & sports STINKS

It's hard to always do the right thing and live by God's rules. It's hard to take our eyes off what we think we need and trust God to provide what we really need. In a beautiful passage from the book of Matthew, Jesus reminds us that God does understand our needs:

> *Therefore I tell you, do not worry about your life, what you will eat or drink; or about your body, what you will wear. Is not life more important than food, and the body more important than clothes? Look at the birds of the air; they do not sow or reap or store away in barns, and yet your heavenly Father feeds them. Are you not much more valuable than they? Who of you by worrying can add a single hour to his life?*
>
> *So do not worry, saying, "What shall we eat?" or "What shall we drink?" or "What shall we wear?" For the pagans run after all these things, and your heavenly Father knows that you need them. But seek first his kingdom and his righteousness, and all these things will be given to you as well. (Matthew 6:25–27, 31–33)*

What it comes down to is this:

Do you have enough faith in God to take what he has to give instead of holding onto what he wants you to give up?

I say I am but in reality I am weak I cried about my finger + knew crippled

The Breastplate of Righteousness

A breastplate was a piece of armor which fit like a vest over the chest and back of a soldier, not unlike the bulletproof vest of today. In Bible times, breastplates were made from leather, metal, or a combination of metal rings or strips sewn onto a leather vest. They protected the soldier's most vulnerable organs—the heart and the lungs. Without a breastplate, a soldier in hand-to-hand combat was in great danger of being killed. Even keeping his distance from the enemy, a soldier needed a breastplate to be fully protected from spears and arrows.

Paul said we need to put on righteousness like a breastplate. When we do things God's way instead of giving in to temptations and the desire to conform, we are actually protecting ourselves from Satan's attacks. What are we protected against?

regret   broken relationships   guilt

a ruined reputation   emotional scars

and perhaps much worse

Most of all, we will protect the thing which has the greatest value in our lives: our relationship with God.

Do you believe that? Do you understand what you have to lose if you sacrifice your relationship with God in exchange for a few of the pleasures of life? Here' a list of four things Satan would like very much to snatch away from you:

worry Immobilizes you

Concern brings you to action

(1) Eternal reward:

You've accepted Jesus as your Savior, and you're planning on meeting him in heaven someday. Did you know that the way you live on earth affects the eternal life you will have in heaven?

Jesus told his followers to *"store up for yourselves treasures in heaven, where moth and rust do not destroy, and where thieves do not break in and steal"* (Matthew 6:20). He told a rich man to sell his possessions and give to the poor, *"and you will have treasure in heaven"* (Matthew 19:16-21).

Paul said what we do during our lives is like constructing a building. Sometimes we build with *"gold, silver, costly stones"* and sometimes with *"wood, hay, or straw"* (1 Corinthians 3:12). On the day of judgment, each person's work will be tested by fire. *"If what he has built survives, he will receive his reward"* (1 Corinthians 3:14).

Are you storing up treasure in heaven by living a righteous life?

(2) Knowing God:

Of course, we don't have to wait until we reach heaven to receive a reward, because the best reward is available right now. We can have a close, personal relationship with our God and our Lord Jesus Christ right now.

Are you looking for love, for acceptance, for a good friend who really cares about you? You don't have to look any further than your heavenly Father. Paul tells us that we can cry out to God just like we would cry out to a loving human father. *"For you did not receive a spirit that makes you a slave again to fear, but you received the Spirit of sonship. And by him we cry, 'Abba, Father'"* (Romans 8:15).

But this relationship comes at a cost. Jesus said, *"You are my friends if you do what I command"* (John 15:14). And John wrote, *"We know that we have come to know him if we obey his commands"* (1 John 2:3). The assurance that God is with us and that God is for us comes as a natural result of following after God with our whole hearts.

Are you getting to know Jesus right now by living a righteous life?

(3) A life of purpose:

Do you want to live a life that matters? Do you want to make a difference? Do you want to come to the end of your days here on earth knowing your time and your gifts were not wasted? The only sure way to do that is to stick with the Man with the Master Plan.

God says: *"I know the plans I have for you...plans to prosper you and not to harm you, plans to give you hope and a future"* (Jeremiah 29:11). We are promised that *"he who began a good work in you will carry it on to completion until the day of Christ Jesus"* (Philippians 1:6). *"For it is God who works in you to will and to act according to his good purpose"* (Philippians 2:13).

Only by finding and following God's will can we be assured that we have a life that matters, for *"God is able to make all grace abound to you, so that in all things at all times, having all that you need, you will abound in every good work"* (2 Corinthians 9:8).

God wants to give you a life full of purpose and meaning; are you ready to live a life of righteousness for him?

(4) Reaching others:

Many Christians are afraid of being *too* good because they think other people won't like them and they might be turned off to the good news of the gospel. To some extent that might be true. If you try to do the right things and say no to all the wrong things, your "goodness" is going to make other people look bad, and they don't like that. People don't want a constant reminder that they aren't living up to God's expectations, and they don't want you to judge them. Because of this, many Christians downplay the whole righteous living thing and just talk about God's love and forgiveness.

But the truth is, nobody is going to listen to you about the love of God until they see proof that your God is real. The most effective evidence you can give them that God is real is that he is making a difference in your life—in the way you feel, in the way you think, and in the way you act. What really impresses people is not our talk about God's love, but that we live by God's law. And Love

Jesus said:

> *"You are the light of the world. A city on a hill cannot be hidden. Neither do people light a lamp and put it under a bowl. Instead they put it on its stand, and it gives light to everyone in the house. In the same way, let your light shine before men, that they may see your good deeds and praise your Father in heaven"* (Matthew 5:14–16)

we are light for the world

Your light of righteousness may make other people feel uncomfortable, but it's the only way they will really know what the gospel is all about.

Are you willing to put people off a little by living a righteous life? It just might be the thing that convinces them that God is real.

> Are you unsure what it means to be righteous? Look up Mark 12:28-34 and write out the two most important commandments here:
>
> *heart, soul, mind & strength*
>
> *Love your neighbour as yourself*

Still not convinced? Do the lures of Satan's temptations and the fear of the opinion of others still have a strong hold on you? After all, you have your whole life ahead of you to be "righteous" and to store up treasure in heaven. Why not enjoy a little fun now?

There is one more thing Satan wants to take from you, and that is time.

> ➢ *Now is the time* God wants you to be drawing close to him.
> ➢ *Now is the time* he wants you to lay a foundation of righteousness your whole life can be built on.
> ➢ *Now is the time* he wants to use you to make a difference in this world.
> ➢ *Today is the day* you can build up treasure in heaven instead of enjoying that which is *"meaningless, a chasing after the wind"* (Ecclesiastes 2:11).
> ➢ *Today is the day* Satan wants to take you out of the game because he knows just how much you can achieve if you live God's way, in God's power.

bless Church Church – Bible Bro Men

don't anything going Steal my joy

49

It's up to you to choose.

Let your light shine before men, that they may see your good deeds and praise your Father in heaven.

Matthew 5:14–16

A Final Word

I started this chapter by talking about a spiritual tightrope. There are so many people in this world living day to day, wondering if they are good enough to get into heaven, wondering on which side of the tightrope they will fall when their lives on earth are over. Aren't you glad you don't have to live like that? The grace of God, through the sacrifice of his Son, has provided a safety net below you that will catch you no matter how many times you fail in this life. Knowing that net is there can lead some people to ignore God's commands for their lives and take off their spiritual armor. It inspires other people to take real risks in life and to follow God with their whole hearts.

That reminds me of another tightrope story:

A daredevil once stood on a rooftop in front of a rope stretched over a busy city street to the roof of another building. He asked the crowd that gathered if they believed he could cross the rope to the other side. They said, yes, they believed! He asked if they believed he could push a wheelbarrow across the rope and get to the other side. They said, yes, they believed! He asked if anyone believed in him enough to get in the wheelbarrow and go with him to the other side. Strangely enough, no one answered. "That, my friends," he told them, "is the difference between belief and trust."

How much do you *trust* Jesus? Enough to get in the wheelbarrow and really give your life to him?

Consider:

Look up Philippians 3:7–9, and write it out below. Then consider the following questions:

What have you given up for the sake of Jesus Christ? Has it been worth it? If you're not sure, you may need to talk it over with God. Ask him to increase your love—for him and for others—so your righteousness will flow as a natural result of your relationship with him. Ask him to help you trust that what he has planned for your life is so much better than what you could ever hope to achieve alone.

Is there something in your life you know you should give up for the sake of Jesus Christ? God has promised so many times in his Word that he will reward those who are faithful and obedient to him. **Do you trust him? Do you trust him enough to change your life and live for him?**

Philippians 3:7-9: *Whatever gains I have I now Consider a Loss b/c of Christ More Than That I now Consider Every Thing a loss because of Christ*

write out

And Look Up:

Philippians 1:6: The one who began the good work in you will continue to complete it until the day of Christ Jesus

Philippians 2:13: In God is the one who for his good purpose MARKS works in you both for desire and to work

2 Corinthians 9:8: The behaviour to which he exhorts them is grounded in Gods own pattern of behaviour

The good news is that we don't have to try to be good and righteous all our own! God has a purpose for each one of us and will help us do all he wants us to do.

Apply:

Satan's Big Guns are temptation—doing what pleases me—and conformity—doing what pleases others. This week, pay attention to decisions you make and ask if you are choosing to do what pleases you, what pleases others, or what pleases God. At least once a day, make a note on one of the doors on the next page about a choice you made that day. What rewards did you expect to find behind that door?

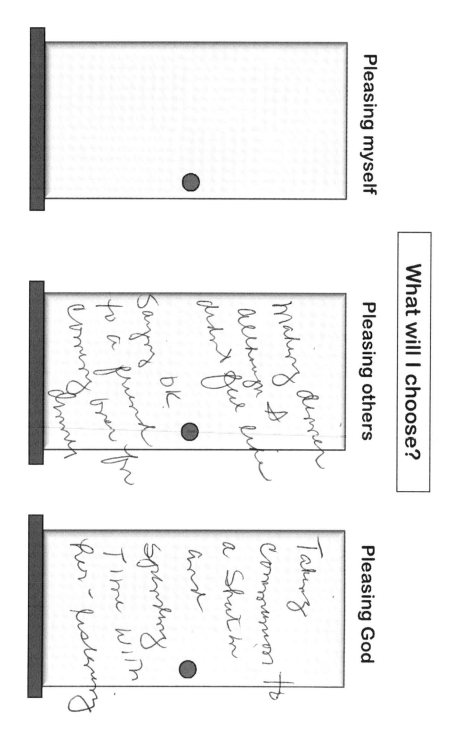

5

THE GOSPEL OF PEACE

In the early morning hours of June 6, 1944, nearly 2,000 ships carrying 120,000 soldiers from five nations waited off the coast of France, ready to launch the most significant assault of World War II. The battle for the beaches of Normandy lasted throughout the day and into the night and cost the Allies some 5,000 lives, but it punched a hole in the Germans' defenses that eventually led to their defeat and an end to the war in Europe.

The sheer size of the invasion was almost unbelievable. Never before had so many troops been delivered by sea into enemy territory—and the odds of something going wrong were very high. Ernie Pyle, a war correspondent, overheard one soldier telling his commanding officer about his fears:

> "Sir, I took my little black dog with me in my arms and I sure was scared standing in that assault boat. Finally we hit the beach and as we piled out into the water we were worse scared than ever. Then we waded ashore and looked around and there right ahead of me was a white house just where you said it would be and after that I wasn't scared." (Ernie Pyle, *Brave Men*, 1943)

It's amazing to think of this young man on the verge of a great battle in the middle of a great war suddenly finding a sense of peace. We usually think of war and peace as being extreme opposites with no possibility of existing in the same place at the same time. Yet in the list of battle armor Paul tells us to put on in Ephesians 6, he mentions having our "feet fitted with the readiness that comes from the gospel of peace."

That's right. We're supposed to have peace, and use it in our spiritual battles!

Obviously, Paul didn't mean we should try to make peace with our enemy. Satan has no intentions of making peace with us, not unless we, and all of God's forces, make a complete surrender to him. That's just not going to happen. Paul isn't saying we should "Make Peace, Not War!" But in the *middle* of our spiritual war with Satan and his forces, somehow we're supposed to find peace and strap it to our feet!

> ? What do you think of when you hear the word peace?
> Make a mental picture of yourself at peace.

(handwritten margin notes: "Rest is worry or fright", "Rest", "worry")

What is Peace?

When we think of the Bible and the word "peace," we are likely to picture the scene of shepherds guarding their sheep by night. Suddenly, an angel appears with good news about a baby in a manger, then a multitude of angels join in singing,

"Glory to God in the highest, and on earth *peace*, goodwill to men."

Perhaps you've been in a Christmas pageant as a shepherd or an angel. You have undoubtedly sung a carol or two about that big night. We hear about it every Christmas: peace on earth. Only it's usually capitalized: *Peace on Earth!* We sing about it. We pray for it. Peace on Earth: an end to wars, an end to bitterness and hostility, an end to fear.

But the wars go on. Bitter struggles which have lasted for centuries continue. We find new ways to kill, new things to be afraid of. The Christmas ideal of peace on earth seems to be nothing more than an oasis in the midst of a violent world—or maybe it's just a mirage.

Did the angels get it wrong? Or have we been wrong in our understanding of what the angels pronounced? Were they announcing a peace which would come sometime in the future, when all wars would end and everybody would live harmoniously with everybody else? Or were they perhaps talking about a different kind of peace, the opposite of a different kind of war?

If you remember from the second chapter of this book, Satan and God have been at war since the beginning of time, and every one of us—every human who lives on the earth—is on one side of the conflict or the other, God's side or Satan's. When you became a Christian you switched sides in the Great War and joined God's forces. **You are no longer at war with God. He has offered you peace.**

Unfortunately, peace with God means you are now at war with Satan and all his forces. So our peace is not yet complete. It won't be complete until Satan is defeated and removed from the earth.

Perhaps that's what the angels meant, that because of Jesus' birth we can find peace with God and eventually complete peace will reign after Satan is defeated. But I think there's something more to the peace God offers than just an end of war and conflict. It means more than just the lack of commotion and difficulties. It promises something more than the absence of fear.

Jesus didn't come to earth just to take our problems away. He came to stand with us in the midst of our problems so we would find that he, himself, *is* our *peace*.

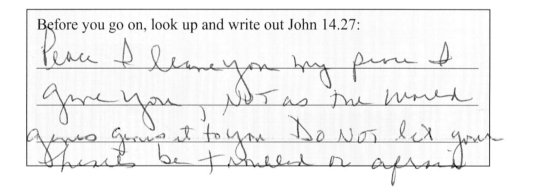

Before you go on, look up and write out John 14.27:

Peace I leave you my peace I give you, not as the world gives it to you. Do not let your spirits be troubled or afraid

Satan's Works of Sabotage

Throughout history, people have thought of many ways to wage a war. Some battles take place face-to-face with the enemy. Others involve dropping bombs or shooting missiles at far off targets. Snipers hide behind cover and shoot at people who are out in the open. Minefields and IEDs slow troops who are trying to take new land. Or a secret agent might sneak behind the lines of battle and sabotage the weapons or equipment of the enemy while no one is looking.

STANDING FIRM – CHAPTER FIVE

Sabotage is destruction or damage done covertly and behind enemy lines. It usually involves the destruction of equipment that is needed for battle, or it might involve damaging roads, airports, or means of communication. The idea is to prevent or delay needed forces and equipment from getting to the front lines where the battle is taking place.

When we join forces with God and make peace with him through the sacrifice of Jesus Christ, Satan tries to sabotage that peace. He can't drag us back out of God's family, but he can mess up the relationship we have with God. He can cause us to doubt God's love or power. He can distract us away from relying on God. He can even enlist us as double agents and get us to sabotage other Christians as well. And being very good at covert operations, he can do a lot of damage without us even knowing he's there.

Satan has an endless supply of tricks and traps to damage our effectiveness as God's soldiers. He uses them to slow us down, keep us off balance, and maybe stop us altogether.

The word *sabotage* has only been used for about a hundred years to refer to secretive damage done during a war or other disputes. Before the word became associated with battle tactics, it was used to mean doing something badly, ruining something, or just messing it up. It's an Old French word that originally meant "old boot," "old shoe," or perhaps "wooden shoe." The mental image it created was of someone fumbling about in noisy boots, two sizes too big, and making a mess of everything in her path.

It's interesting that Paul tells us to put the gospel of peace on our feet, when Satan would rather see us in oversized, uncomfortable shoes we can't do anything in.

On a recent family vacation, I was reminded of how important it is to have good shoes. Shoes that don't fit right can rub and rub until we have a big blister or an open sore. If they're too big, they let in irritating rocks and sand. If they're too small, they pinch and cramp. If they're too thin, they offer no protection for our feet at all. Even a little irritation of our feet can slow us down, keep us off balance, and maybe even stop us completely— exactly the kinds of things Satan wants to do with our spiritual lives.

So what is Satan doing to sabotage us? What are the rubbing, pinching, rocks in our shoes he uses to keep us distracted from the battle? Take a look at this list and see if any of these have ever stopped you from living the life God wants you to live: (HURT)

Shame   (Anger)   **Doubt**   **Guilt**   **Fear**   (**Disappointment**)   **Bitterness**

Frustration   **Loneliness**   **Sorrow**   **Envy**   **Emptiness**

Each of the items on this list is an emotion common to all people. It's natural to feel angry when someone insults us or to feel guilty when we've done something wrong. It's good to fear things that can hurt us, and doubt in our minds may be the voice of reason we should listen to.

But each of these things, like badly fitting shoes, can continue to rub and rub until we're too sore to keep going. If we dwell on our negative emotions and keep wearing them on our feet, they're going to do some serious damage. And that's just what Satan wants!

fear is the opposite of faith

Bad feelings may be a natural part of life, but God never intended for his children to be sidelined by them.

The Bible tells us to *"get rid of all bitterness, rage and anger"* (Ephesians 4:31). Jesus told his disciples to *"stop doubting and believe"* (John 20:27). And the words *"Do not be afraid"* are found at least 80 times in the Bible. God said it, angels said it, prophets said it, and Jesus said it—repeatedly! The reason why we should not be afraid is made clear, too: *"For the Lord your God will be with you wherever you go"* (Joshua 1:9).

> ? What are some negative emotions you've been struggling with? Go back to the last page and circle any that apply.

Feet Fitted with the Gospel of Peace

Paul tells us the secret to protecting ourselves against negative emotions and the damage they can cause when he tells us to have our *"feet fitted with the readiness that comes from the gospel of peace"* (Ephesians 6:15). Although the word *"peace"* can be found more than 150 times in the Bible, this phrase, *"the gospel of peace,"* is used nowhere else in the Old or New Testaments. Paul didn't explain it, and he didn't tell us how putting it on our feet is supposed to help us in our spiritual battles, but I think we can figure out what he was talking about.

The word "gospel" means "good news" or "good tidings." Remember that phrase? The angel who came to the shepherds said, *"Do not be afraid. I bring you **good news** of great joy that will be for all the people"* (Luke

2:10). The angel came to announce the *gospel*, the good news that Jesus had come into the world.

But the good news doesn't end with the Christmas story. Jesus taught us how to know God and how to serve him, he showed us how to love each other, and then he gave his own life as a sacrifice for our sins so we could live with him someday in heaven.

And the good news doesn't end with Easter. Jesus is living in heaven right now, watching over us. The Holy Spirit lives within us to help us know God better and to experience his love. God has a plan for your life, and he has a plan for the whole world. In the end, everything will work out according to his plan, and he—and we—will be victorious.

That's good news!

Remembering that good news every day—preaching ourselves the gospel, putting it on our feet and standing on it—is our protection from Satan's attempts to sabotage our lives. How can we doubt God's love for us when we remember that Jesus died for us? How can we be afraid of the future when God is in control and has promised us victory in Christ? How can we be angry at what other people have done to us when God has forgiven all our sins against him? He sent his own Son to die, to pay the penalty for those sins.

> **He who did not spare his own Son, but gave him up for us all—how will he not also, along with him, graciously give us all things?**
>
> **Romans 8:32**

When we look at what God has done, at who God is, at what he has promised us—when we remember the good news of the gospel—our perspective changes and the doubts, fears, and hurts which have been rubbing us the wrong way just disappear. It's like taking off a pair of noisy boots, two sizes too big, and putting on a pair of comfortable sneakers.

Does that sound too simple? Too difficult? Maybe you're thinking it isn't so easy to let go of your anger, your hurts, or your fear. Maybe you have good reasons to be angry or there are real things in your life that are very scary. After all, who am I to tell you how to live your life? I don't know you. I don't know about the issues you have to face every day.

You're right, of course. There may be a lot of people who read this book whom I can't relate to at all. There's an old proverb that says you shouldn't judge another person until you've walked a mile in their shoes. So I won't tell you what *I* think, or what *I* know. I'll let someone else do the talking.

If you've been the victim of prejudice, verbal abuse, violence, betrayal, or even the results of your own bad choices, there's one man who could really relate. His name was Paul, and this is what he had to say about his life:

For I am the least of the apostles and do not even deserve to be called an apostle, because I persecuted the church of God. (1 Corinthians 15:9)

Five times I received from the Jews the forty lashes minus one. Three times I was beaten with rods, once I was stoned, three times I was shipwrecked, I spent a night and a day in the open sea, I have been constantly on the move. I have been in danger from rivers, in danger from bandits, in danger from my own countrymen, in danger from Gentiles; in danger in the city, in danger in the country, in danger at sea; and in danger from false brothers. I have labored and toiled and have often gone without sleep; I have known hunger and thirst and have often gone without food; I have been cold and naked. (2 Corinthians 11:24–27)

We do not want you to be uninformed, brothers, about the hardships we suffered in the province of Asia. We were under great pressure, far beyond our ability to endure, so that we despaired even of life. Indeed, in our hearts we felt the sentence of death. But this happened that we might not rely on ourselves but on God, who raises the dead. He has delivered us from such a deadly peril, and he will deliver us. On him we have set our hope that he will continue to deliver us. (2 Corinthians 1:8–10)

But we have this treasure in jars of clay to show that this all-surpassing power is from God and not from us. We are hard pressed on every side, but not crushed; perplexed, but not in despair; persecuted, but not abandoned; struck down, but not destroyed. We always carry around in our body the death of Jesus, so that the life of Jesus may also be revealed in our body. (2 Corinthians 4:7–10)

And we know that in all things God works for the good of those who love him, who have been called according to his purpose. (Romans 8:28)

That is why, for Christ's sake, I delight in weaknesses, in insults, in hardships, in persecutions, in difficulties. For when I am weak, then I am strong. (2 Corinthians 12:10)

Like the soldier on the beach of Normandy, Paul didn't find peace in the absence of problems; he found hope, faith, and peace *in the midst* of terrible circumstances. It was there he saw God working and realized that everything was under God's control—and God was doing all these things for Paul's own good!

This is the best part of the good news of the gospel. It's not that God will make our lives safe, happy, and prosperous all the time when we put our trust in him. It's that, **when we put our trust in him, everything that does happen in our life—every good, bad, exciting, exasperating, beautiful, terrible thing that happens—is for our good.**

These things happen to make us into the people God wants us to be. They happen so we will rely on God alone for our strength, our hope, and our joy. And the more we rely on God and trust him to use everything for our good, the more we find ourselves at peace in a world that is full of turmoil and hatred and war.

It isn't easy to trust God this way. It takes a lot of practice, living through a lot of difficult experiences, trying and failing and trying again. But we can get there. Paul had one more thing to say about this kind of peace:

> *I have learned to be content whatever the circumstances. I know what it is to be in need, and I know what it is to have plenty. I have learned the secret of being content in any and every situation, whether well fed or hungry, whether living in plenty or in want. I can do everything through him who gives me strength.* Philippians 4:11–13

Not long after writing these words, Paul was executed by the Romans because of his work for the gospel.

I don't think he was afraid. I'm sure he had peace.

we must to learn to be content

A Final Word

I don't want you to think from what I've just said that God wants you to be a happy, smiling automaton that never experiences any negative emotions. There are times when those emotions will overwhelm us for a while until we remember the Gospel of Peace and strap it on again.

There are even times when those emotions are appropriate and useful: The Bible tells us to *fear* the Lord our God, to never forget his awesome power and his hatred for sin. We should *hate* the sin in our own lives and try to get rid of it. We should *grieve* for the sin in the lives of people we know and share with them the good news of God's forgiveness. We should feel *guilty* when we have unconfessed sin in our lives and *sorrowful* when we haven't done all we could to repair the damage we've done to someone else. We should be *angry* when Christian leaders misuse God's Word or abuse their power, and we should confront them about it the way Jesus confronted the Pharisees of his time.

This is a war we're in, and being a good soldier requires serious, careful thinking—not happy, sunny, all-is-good-with-the-world blinders. But even on the front line of the battle we can move forward without fear, suffering harm without anger, and doing our work without doubt, because we are not alone.

If you have trouble letting go of negative emotions that are tripping you up or holding you back, don't give up. We have to put on our shoes every day, and we have to remind ourselves of the gospel every day, too. Like breaking in new shoes, it may take a while before it feels right. But it will if you just keep trusting.

Consider:

Compare the list of negative emotions on page 60 to the circumstances Paul wrote about on pages 64-65. Could Paul have suffered from any of these emotions? Instead of dwelling on negative emotions, what did Paul focus on? How can we encourage one another to stay focused on the good news of the gospel instead of on the negative things in our lives? Think of some specific actions and make a commitment to help each other stay focused on God.

Sometimes reading about people in the Bible can seem like reading about characters in a fairy tale. It helps me to read and think about people in more modern times who have gone through terrible circumstances who have not only kept their faith in God but found it to be deeper and richer. Two of my favorite Christian role models are Corrie Ten Boom (author of *The Hiding Place* and many other books) and Gladys Aylward, missionary to China. Among your group, share some of your Christian role models. If you have books about these Christian heroes, why not share them or offer them to your church library to inspire others?

Look Up:

Joshua 1:9: _____

_____

_____

John 16:33: _____

_____

_____

Philippians 4:19: *And my God will supply*
every riches + new acts

Apply:

Keep a journal this week about your negative emotions. Are you dealing with fear, anger, disappointment, or some other bad feeling? What does God have to say about those feelings? Write a sentence about the negative emotions and what you think is causing them. Then write a sentence about the good news you have in Jesus. Include an encouraging Bible verse from this chapter or find one for yourself. Then ask yourself, do you believe it? Do you believe it enough to let go of the negative emotions and trust God to use even these circumstances for good?

There are a few lined pages at the back of this book you can use for this journal or for other notes.

6

THE SHIELD OF FAITH

I always liked the short story *The Lady or the Tiger*, by Frank Stockman. It's an unusual story because it doesn't have an ending. You have to think about the story and finish it yourself. If you've never read the story or can't remember how it goes, let me give a synopsis of it:

In a semi-barbaric kingdom long ago, a young man had the great nerve to fall in love with the king's daughter, who loved him in return. Put on trial for the crime of loving the princess, the man was sent into an arena to determine his fate. He had to choose one of two doors. Behind one was a ferocious tiger; behind the other was a beautiful maiden to whom he would be instantly married.

Although one fate was considered a punishment for guilt and the other a reward for innocence, the king was pleased to know either result would keep the young man from pursuing his daughter any longer. The princess realized this as well, and she hated the idea of her lover being married to another woman. Unhappy about either outcome, the princess found out which door led to the tiger and which to the woman, as the young man was sure she would. Standing before the king and a great crowd seated in the arena, the young man looked to the princess to indicate which door he should choose. She pointed to the right, and her lover went instantly to that door and opened it.

Which came out, the lady or the tiger?

The story doesn't tell us but leaves the reader to decide. What kind of woman was the princess? Would she send her lover to his death or into the arms of another woman? And what kind of man was he to trust her so completely and go to the door she indicated without a second thought? Is it wise to put so much confidence in one person? Would it be any wiser to simply trust to fate and open a door at random?

When your very life depends upon making the right decision, is there anyone or anything in which you can have complete faith?

Faith is a hot topic today. As our world grows ever smaller, we discover more and more people who have beliefs different from our own. Some people believe in fate, others in family or country. Some read their horoscopes religiously; others trust in the power of their own positive thoughts. There are many different religions and many different beliefs within each religion and denomination. It's hard to know what to believe, whom to trust, or where to put your faith. We're even told by some people that it's best not to trust anyone too much. You can really rely only on yourself.

How very sad it is, because in the midst of all the choices and possibilities, all the doctrine, superstitions, crackpot beliefs, and homespun wisdom, there is something real we can believe in—something that has power, not because we believe in it, but because it's true whether we believe in it or not.

It's not a reality of our making, something we can bend to our own desires or make into whatever we want. It's what we've been talking about through this whole book: It's **God—his truth, his power, his plan, and his love!** These are the things you can trust and put your faith in. He is the one you can bet your life on.

The next item of spiritual armor Paul tells us to take up is the shield of faith (Ephesians 6:16). It takes faith to become a Christian and join God's army in the first place (Ephesians 2:8), and it takes faith to keep our hearts and minds protected from the assaults of our enemy, Satan.

What is Faith?

Most people think of faith as something which comes from within us— a conscious or unconscious decision to trust someone or to believe in something. Many people think their belief can empower the object of their belief. If they just believe hard enough, they can make things happen. "Believe in yourself!" "Believe in your dreams!" "You have to believe it to receive it!"

There may be some truth to the positive thoughts and positive attitudes teachings you hear about today, but for the most part, they're ridiculous.

I can't make myself fly by believing I can. I can't make myself happy and healthy just by dreaming about it. And you can't make yourself a famous pop star or a wealthy athlete just because you wish for it with all your heart.

Faith, belief, and confidence are only as good as the things in which we put our faith.

I like to use the following analogy. You can believe that a chair is going to hold your weight without breaking and dropping you to the ground. That seems reasonable enough. You can also believe the chair is not only going to support your weight and keep you from falling but is also going to save you from dying. It's a nice, comfortable belief, but it probably isn't going to work. Your belief doesn't empower the chair to save you. It's just a chair, made to support your weight without breaking and dropping you to the ground. And if it isn't a well-made chair, it isn't even going to do that, no matter how much you believe it will.

As for any particular chair, you can believe with your whole heart that it will hold your weight and not drop you to the ground, but you will never know for sure it will unless you sit on it, put your weight on it, and let it hold you. *It* holding *you*. Not you holding it. That's faith. Only when you put your weight on it do you find out if the chair is *faithful*—capable of performing the job you trust it to do. When the chair is faithful, you can have faith in it. The more times you test the chair and find it faithful, the more faith in it you have.

The Bible defines faith this way: *"Now faith is being sure of what we hope for and certain of what we do not see"* (Hebrews 11:1). We can be sure and certain of God's love and truth and power and plan when we trust ourselves to them completely. Only when we rely on God can we find him faithful.

Best friend
even family
husband

> **?** Who or what do you trust to take care of you, to tell you the truth, to help you, or to love you? Are they always faithful?

Satan's Flaming Arrows

Faith is such an important part of the Christian life that Satan is always looking for ways to attack it. We already know he uses lies and temptations to turn us away from God. He tempts us to disobey God and please ourselves and others. He can sabotage our peace with God by getting us to dwell on painful emotions. And, as we'll see in the next chapter, he bombards us with worldly propaganda to take our thoughts away from God. But he also delights in attacking our personal image, what many would call "self–esteem," to keep us from giving our all to God.

Paul tells us: *Take up the shield of faith, with which you can extinguish all the flaming arrows of the evil one* (Ephesians 6:16).

group

Have you had any flaming arrows winging your way lately?

Emunah
hebrew
word
faith

Think for a moment about the things that really sting and burn you—the words, the looks, the actions other people send your way which just plain hurt. Insults wound us and rejection stings. Being put down, passed over, or laughed at by other people is very painful. And when it's a Christian who's in pain, Satan sits back and chalks up a victory for his side, because all too often we let the pain of our personal injuries turn us away from God instead of sending us running to him.

> When was the last time you were insulted, laughed at, or rejected? Are you still hurting from that experience? Write a sentence or two about a particularly painful time in your life when your self-confidence was under attack:
>
> _Recently someone said: Her Name is Roseanne. How awful. She must be teased a lot about that. Roseanne Danna Roseanne Danna Poor thing_

Sometimes, we're the ones damaging our own self-image. We compare ourselves to others in looks, popularity, abilities, and the stuff we own. We constantly feel the pressure of knowing that someone else is better looking, smarter, funnier, richer, better at sports, getting more attention—the list goes on and on. And it's just human nature to rub it in to the people not as good looking, smart, funny, or popular as we are. We make snide remarks about them, leave them out, or even push them around. It's no wonder so many people today have poor self-esteem. _Starting to feel OLD — FAT matronly_

So what's the answer? How can we feel good about ourselves when we're surrounded by people who keep telling us we're not good enough? _Amen_

Or you might ask, are we even supposed to feel good about ourselves? The Bible says we should be *poor in spirit* (Matthew 5:3) and *humble* (Ephesians 4:2) and that we should *consider others better than ourselves* (Philippians 2:3).

All of you, clothe yourselves with humility toward one another, because, 'God opposes the proud but gives grace to the humble.' (1 Peter 5:5)

Being puffed up with pride in ourselves, our abilities, and our accomplishments isn't a good Christian way to live, but who wants to be meek, low, or inferior—all synonyms for humble? It's a tough issue to get around, but there is a simple answer: Our confidence should not be in ourselves but in God!

Now faith is being sure of what we hope for and certain [or **confident***] of what we do not see.* (Hebrews 11:1)

Such **confidence** *as this is ours through Christ before God. Not that we are competent in ourselves to claim anything for ourselves, but our competence comes from God.* (2 Corinthians 3:4–5)

In him and through faith in him we may approach God with freedom and **confidence***.* (Ephesians 3:12)

Being **confident** *of this, that he who began a good work in you will carry it on to completion until the day of Christ Jesus.* (Philippians 1:6)

Let us then approach the throne of grace with **confidence***, so that we may receive mercy and find grace to help us in our time of need.* (Hebrews 4:16)

So we say with **confidence***, "The Lord is my helper; I will not be afraid. What can man do to me?"* (Hebrews 13:6)

Maybe you have great self-confidence, or maybe you measure yourself against the people around you and keep coming up short. Either way, what you're putting your faith in is going to let you down.

Only when you put your faith in God and fully rely on him will you ever find something that is solid, unwavering, and always, always faithful.

> **?** When you don't feel good enough, or smart enough, or pretty enough, or popular enough, how can the verses on the last page help you overcome your self-doubts?

The Shield of Faith

Faith is such an important part of the Christian walk that Paul could have called the spiritual armor in Ephesians 6 the *armor of faith* instead of the *armor of God*. We are called to be faithful to the truth (3 John 1:3). Our righteousness comes from faith (Romans 1:17; Philippians 3:9). We have peace with God because we have been justified by faith (Romans 5:1). And best of all, we are promised VICTORY through faith:

> *For everyone born of God overcomes the world. This is the victory that has overcome the world, even our faith.* (1 John 5:4)

It's no wonder Paul added faith to his list of protective armor, along with truth, righteousness, and peace. He calls it the *"shield of faith, with which you can extinguish all the flaming arrows of the evil one"* (Ephesians 6:16).

There were two basic types of shields used by Roman soldiers in Paul's day. One was a small shield, usually round, which was used in hand-to-hand combat. The other was a large, rectangular shield used by soldiers walking together into battle. These large shields were made of wood or metal and often covered in leather. The leather could be soaked in water to help defend the soldier against a common attack—flaming arrows. The large shield protected most of the body of the soldier, and the wet leather extinguished the fiery darts of the enemy.

The shield was an extra layer of protection, used in addition to helmets, breastplates, and heavy belts. It was the first layer of protection, which stood between the soldier and his enemy.

> *Through faith [we] are **shielded** by God's power until the coming of the salvation that is ready to be revealed in the last time"* (1 Peter 1:5).

> *The Lord is my strength and my **shield**; my heart trusts in him, and I am helped"* (Psalm 28:7).

When we have faith in God—fully relying on him for protection from harm and for our purpose in life, our peace, and our happiness—we stop looking at ourselves and our own weaknesses. We stop looking to others to tell us if we're good or bad, ugly or attractive, successful or unsuccessful.

God's love becomes our standard.

We are the people Jesus died to save. We are the friends of God. We are the elect who will someday walk the streets of gold in heaven. We are loved, cared for, directed, disciplined for our own good, and called to stand with God in the work he wants to do in this world.

And the best part is he will supply everything we need (2 Corinthians 9:8), so we never have to rely on our own abilities or even our own obedience. During those times when we lose our grip on the truth, or when we aren't living a righteous life, or we fail to guard our emotions or our thoughts, faith is still there like a shield in front of us, protecting us from the worst of Satan's attacks.

A Final Word

There is another important thing you should know about the shield Paul wrote about. The large battle shield was developed to be used by soldiers standing next to each other, in close formation. Each shield protected the soldier who carried it and the soldier standing by his side.

When the army stood close together, almost shoulder to shoulder, the shields joined together to form an almost impenetrable defense. Ancient armies would literally walk into each other, first using spears to try to penetrate the enemy's defenses and then just pushing into each other, shield against shield. When one army broke through the other's line of shields it was nearly certain they would win the battle.

In ancient times, battles were not won by valiant soldiers slashing away at each other with swords or by daring heroes riding around on white horses. They were won by staying together, keeping the line of defense strong, and marching forward until the enemy gave way.

No matter how strong your individual walk with God may be, you cannot hold out against the forces of Satan on your own. In addition to taking up armor to protect ourselves against Satan's attacks, we are called to stand side-by-side with our brothers and sisters in Christ and guard them as well (1 Corinthians 12:25–26). Not every Christian is strong enough in their faith to put up a good defense, so those who are more mature have to step up to the front line and let others stand behind them until they, too, are ready.

The people who stand with you in this spiritual war, shield to shield, are not just your family and your friends at church. God's army includes people of all ages, from different types of churches, from all over the world. The person standing next to you today guarding your side spiritually may be your spouse, your pastor, or a good friend. It might be someone from work, a neighbor, or someone at church you've never even spoken to who has been praying for you without your knowledge. You, in return, can stand beside a Christian friend—or even someone you don't know—by praying for them and by offering encouragement, assistance, and godly wisdom.

Consider:

Is your confidence in yourself, in God, or in something else? Think about the last time you were attacked by the flaming arrows of criticism, complaints, or rejection. Did you defend yourself by putting others down? Did you give up, turn back, or descend into depression? Did you run to someone else who would tell you how great you are? Or did you turn to God for comfort and help?

Do you think of yourself as a confident person? If yes, are you relying on yourself and your own resources to handle the difficulties of life, or are you relying on God? If no, are you really trusting God like the Bible says you can? Reread the verses on page 76 and then ask yourself: What is one thing you might be willing to do—that you haven't had the courage to do—if you really trusted God to take care of you?

Look up:

Look up and write out 1 Peter 1:3-7, a passage we discussed in the first chapter. Circle the word "faith" each time it occurs: _P. 1878_

1 Peter 1:3-7: _____

_____

_____

_____

_____

_____

_____

_____

_____

_____

_____

Genuous of faith - more precious than gold

_____

_____

> **Since we have been justified through faith, we have peace with God through our Lord Jesus Christ. Romans 5:1**

Apply:

Among the people around you, how many do you know to be Christians? What can you do to encourage and help them in their spiritual battles?

This week, be on the lookout for fellow soldiers in God's army. Make a list of seven Christians you know and pray for one each day. Ask God to strengthen their faith and renew their confidence in who they are in Christ. And as you pray for and care about other Christians, I think you'll find yourself thinking about your own problems less and less. Satan's flaming arrows just can't penetrate a united front of believers standing behind their shields of faith! That's something you can really trust.

1. _____

2. _____

3. _____

4. _____

5. _____

6. _____

7. _____

7

THE HELMET OF SALVATION

Have you ever noticed all the advertising surrounding us? During a one hour TV show I watched last week, I counted 45 commercials! Some were for other TV shows or upcoming events. But most of the commercials were advertising something for sale. I saw commercials telling me to buy cleaning products to kill all those nasty germs in my house, and beauty products to make myself look younger and more attractive, and food commercials aimed at kids which didn't say much about the products they were selling except they come in colorful boxes with a prize inside.

Sunday newspapers used to be filled with advertisements. I once counted 50 advertisement flyers with 442 pages of ads and 80 pages of coupons. In the paper itself, there were more than 300 ads—not including the hundreds of classified listings put in by individuals selling houses, cars, furniture, and services. I'm sure it would take the annual budget of a small nation to pay for everything offered for sale in that one Sunday paper.

My local shopping mall has 148 stores, 32 restaurants, 26 kiosks, and a 20-screen movie theater. Ads in windows or other displays invite shoppers to buy clothes, jewelry, books, music, cell phones, and even houses. Add to that all the goods displayed in store windows which do their advertising without words, and the whole mall experience is nothing but a nonstop, surround-sound commercial telling you to buy, buy, buy!

Anything you can buy in stores can now be bought online as well. Amazon offers hundreds of millions of items for sale, and that's just one of thousands of retail and resale shopping sites online.

Of course, television, newspapers, shopping malls, and the Internet sell more than stuff we can cart home in bags or boxes. They also sell ideas, styles, prejudices, and expectations. Your ideas about the perfect weight, height, and hairstyle probably come from the shows and commercials you watch on TV. What you know about the world, about other countries and cultures, is probably due more to what you watch on TV than what you have learned from actual experience. Even the Sunday comic pages are filled with political and social ideas someone is trying to sell along with a laugh.

I don't think there's anything in the world that can't be bought for a price somewhere or anything that someone isn't trying to sell. Thanks to the Internet, you're just a click away from buying a genie in a bottle, fake dog poop, an empty paper sack, or a substance guaranteed to make you invisible. I wouldn't be surprised to find someone selling eternal salvation on the Internet, but whatever they're asking for it, it's too much. I know someplace you can get if for free. Is that a bargain or what?

None! They annoy me especially Drug commercials

> ? What are some of your favorite commercials or ads from TV, magazines, or even billboards? What ideas and expectations are they promoting along with the product they're selling?

What is Salvation?

I'm sure it comes as no surprise that there are a lot of people trying to sell you things, whether you need them or not. And you're probably aware that some people want to sell you things they know will hurt you—like drugs, pornography, and other addictions. But did you know that our enemy, Satan, is in the advertising business, too? He wants you to buy into ideas, beliefs, and values designed to destroy your relationship with God.

We are told in Ephesians 6:12 that Satan fights in *"the heavenly realms."* **But here in the earthly realm, we experience that battle the most in our minds.**

In our minds, we struggle with temptation and try to sort through all the lies of our world to find the truth. In our minds, we consciously choose to follow God and have faith in him or else follow some other course and place our faith in ourselves or others. In our minds, we wrestle with our human desires, weaknesses, and failures, and connect with the Spirit of God if we are willing.

If there is any part of our bodies that need protection from Satan's attacks, it is the mind, the brain, the head! It's no wonder, then, that Paul tells us to take up another piece of armor called the helmet of salvation (Ephesians 6:17).

also me Boobs

Usually, when we see the word "salvation" in the Bible it's talking about the work of God, through Jesus Christ, to save us from the penalty of our sins (Acts 4:12, Romans 1:16, 2 Corinthians 7:10, Ephesians 1:13). When Paul tells Christians to take up the helmet of salvation, he isn't saying we need to be saved again from the penalty of our sins. Once we have repented of our sins and accepted Jesus as our Savior, our eternal salvation is assured. But we do need to be saved by God's grace in our daily struggles with Satan, and the most important thing we need to guard and protect in those battles is our mind.

> *For though we live in the world, we do not wage war as the world does. The weapons we fight with are not the weapons of the world. On the contrary, they have divine power to demolish strongholds. We demolish arguments and every pretension that sets itself up against the knowledge of God, and we take captive every thought to make it obedient to Christ.* (2 Corinthians 10:3–5)

> *Those who live according to the sinful nature have their minds set on what that nature desires; but those who live in accordance with the Spirit have their minds set on what the Spirit desires. The mind of sinful man is death, but the mind controlled by the Spirit is life and peace.* (Romans 8:5–6)

"*The mind of sinful man is death*" (Romans 8:6). That's a powerful statement.

The human mind which fails to acknowledge God as the only source of salvation is spiritually dead. But even in the mind of a person saved by God's grace, the poison of sinful thoughts still exists. The extent to which that poison destroys our happiness, our peace, and our potential to live a meaningful life as God's soldiers depends on how much we depend on the grace of God daily to "*take captive every thought*" (2 Corinthians 10:5) and "*live in accordance with the Spirit*" (Romans 8:5).

Satan's Killing Fields

Between 1975 and 1979, a communist group known as the Khmer Rouge controlled the government of the small country of Cambodia in Southeast Asia. To maintain control and to institute a new, highly controlled way of life, the Khmer Rouge outlawed anything to do with the Cambodians' former way of life. They banished schools, churches, banks, hospitals— even families. Children were taken away from their parents and raised in the new thinking of the Khmer Rouge. Anyone who disagreed with the government, or anyone who could be considered a threat to its stability, was brutally murdered.

Around two million Cambodians—almost one-third of the population— died, either at the hands of the Khmer Rouge or as a result of the terrible living conditions which resulted. A great many were taken to large fields where they were killed and buried in shallow graves. Those fields came to be known as "the killing fields."

In 1984, a major motion picture by that name was released to document a small portion of the terrible events in Cambodia. In that story, we see the horrors of war and hate. We see death, brutality, and destruction, and all without any reason we can comprehend. We see evil in human form, the fullest expression of sin and its consequences.

The goal of the Khmer Rouge in Cambodia, like every other Communist government, was to destroy the people's reliance on anything other than the ruling party. They denied the existence of God, destroyed the natural bonds between children and their parents, and removed all traditions and reminders that linked the people to the past. These tactics were not invented by the Communists, however. Satan has been using similar tactics throughout the history of the world. If you pay close attention, you will see that he is using those tactics in our culture today, even in peaceful democracies with traditional Christian foundations.

Tactic #1: Deny or refute the existence of God.

Communism. Evolution. Rationalism. Humanism. Each of these schools of thought teaches that belief in God, or any kind of higher power, is irrational, unscientific, and even harmful. They point to the differences in people's beliefs about God as the cause of many wars and much of the human suffering around the globe from ancient history to modern times. Belief in God, they say, is an outdated relic of the past when humans were unable to explain the universe they lived in without the aid of superstitions and fables. They invite us to let go of the religious beliefs that stifle and handicap us and accept the realities of a godless universe.

Tactic #2: Provide a replacement for God.

Communism replaced God with the State, or the Party, as the thing which demanded the people's loyalty and would provide for their needs. Humanism offers the human race it as the entity we should cherish and the provider of our salvation. Proponents of evolution offer science as the means of solving all our problems. For those less inspired by science or political ideals, our society offers many other things to take our attention and allegiance away from God: fame, wealth, and power for some; traditions, superstitions, and man-made religions for others; and, of course, the all-powerful "me."

Tactic #3: Destroy the bonds between parents and children.

Over the past several decades, our culture has grown more and more youth-oriented, exchanging wisdom and tradition for individual experience. "Question authority" was a big slogan in my high school days. Today, we question everything and are constantly challenged to keep up in a quickly changing world. Parents, who were once the primary source of a child's character development, are now encouraged by society not to impose their values on their children, but rather to let them explore their options and reach their own conclusions about such things as politics, religion, sexual orientation, and even their own gender.

The explosive growth of communication technologies hasn't helped. Most parents and older adults feel completely left behind by a generation of young people texting, blogging, chatting, and living surrogate lives on the Internet. Even in "family-friendly" movies and TV shows, young teens are finding fulfillment in life by turning their backs on the things their parents value. Whether the thing valued is actually good or not, the message is clear: you are responsible for your own happiness, and you shouldn't let your parents stand in the way of your dreams.

It shouldn't surprise us, but each of these strategies is aimed at destroying something God has labeled as valuable and necessary for a good relationship with him. In Exodus 20, we find a list of God's values in the Ten Commandments.

> *"You shall have no other gods before me. You shall not make for yourself an idol in the form of anything in heaven above or on the earth beneath or in the waters below."* In other words, don't let anything stand in as a replacement for God. Give your allegiance to him alone, and don't settle for anything less.

> *"Do not misuse the name of the Lord your God."* How many times a day do you hear that commandment broken? How many times do you break it yourself?

> *"Remember the Sabbath day by keeping it holy."* Don't spend all your time busy with work, family, entertainment, or anything else that keeps your focus off of God.

> *"Honor your father and mother, so that you may live long in the land the Lord your God is giving you."* Don't neglect the values of your parents' generation, and don't let your children and grandchildren neglect you and your beliefs. As parents and grandparents, we may not have all the answers, but we do have life experience worth listening to and learning from.

➤ *"Do not murder"* means we need to respect human life—all of it! The unborn, the terminally ill, the mentally handicapped, even those we consider to be our enemies are deserving of respect as human beings formed in the image of God.

➤ *"Do not commit adultery"* means we should respect the institution of marriage as God designed it and not accept all the easy substitutes our society tells us are okay.

Yes, Satan is very busy keeping up a constant barrage of firepower against God and the things he cares about. As soldiers in God's army, we have to stay alert and keep our minds and hearts protected from those attacks. We need to find a way to be delivered from Satan's killing fields.

> **?** Can you think of specific examples of these tactics being used in your community today?

The Helmet of Salvation

Remember all those advertisements we talked about at the beginning of this chapter? When's the last time you really paid attention to those things? How many times have you looked at a commercial or an ad in a magazine and asked yourself, *What is this ad really saying, and should I believe it?* How many times have you watched a TV show or a movie and wondered, *What is the message here? What is being said about the world I live in?*

In just one night in front of the television you will be bombarded with messages like "The more people you sex have with, the better," "Breaking the rules is the best way to get ahead," "Being vulgar and rude is acceptable

92

and expected," "Be true to yourself, even if it means hurting other people," "Stupid is funny and much more cool than being smart."

You may have heard of the acronym, GIGO. It stands for "garbage in, garbage out." It was thought up by computer programmers who realized the information you put into a computer affects the quality of the information you get back. Put in bad information or leave out something important and the answers the computer gives you won't be accurate. Only when the data provided is accurate and the programming is good will the computer's answer be correct.

The same idea applies to our bodies. Garbage in (foods which are too sugary or fatty or lacking in nutrients), garbage out (obesity, lack of energy, poor health). And it applies to our minds, too. Garbage in (the messages Satan throws at us through our culture), garbage out (lives that are ineffective for God's purpose).

That is why the Bible says,

> *Do not conform any longer to the pattern of this world, but be transformed by the renewing of your mind. Then you will be able to test and approve what God's will is— his good, pleasing and perfect will.* (Romans 12:2)

The secret to controlling and renewing our minds is to fill our minds with the things of God rather than the things of the world.

We need to limit our consumption of messages which turn us away from God, and we need to carefully question the things we do see and hear to determine what messages are hidden, there that are intended to poison our minds against God. Yes, that means actually thinking about what shows we watch on TV, what movies we go to, what books and magazines we read, what games we play, what music we listen to. Satan is using every one of those mediums to spread his doctrine of hate against God and his values. We need to turn completely away from some, limit our exposure to others, and constantly compare the things the world is selling us with the things God says are true.

Therefore, prepare your minds for action; be self–controlled; set your hope fully on the grace to be given you when Jesus Christ is revealed. (1 Peter 1:13)

Finally, brothers, whatever is true, whatever is noble, whatever is right, whatever is pure, whatever is lovely, whatever is admirable—if anything is excellent or praiseworthy—think about such things. Whatever you have learned or received or heard from me, or seen in me—put it into practice. And the God of peace will be with you. (Philippians 4:8–9)

A Final Word

The movie *The Killing Fields* tells the story of an American journalist in Cambodia during the takeover of the Khmer Rouge. As bad as things got there, with bombings, random killings in the streets, and a lack of food and other necessities, the American never completely despaired. Like the other foreigners in the land, he could always go to an embassy for help, hop on a helicopter, or take a truck offering safe passage out of the country. The passports they held proved their citizenship to another country and their right to walk away and leave Cambodia before their worst fears became reality. The American's friend and interpreter, a Cambodian national, was not so lucky. Not until the American had to leave did he realize the full horror of the situation his friend faced.

As Christians, we, too, have citizenship in another kingdom, and our names are on a list guaranteeing us safe passage out of this war zone when the time is right. We live in this world, and we might be very attached to it and not want to leave, but our true home is with God. The situation on this earth is going to grow ever bleaker as Satan, knowing that his time is short, ramps up his battle against God (Revelation 12:12). It is what is different about us—our foreignness, you could say—which is our source of hope in a war-torn world. Please don't trade your passport in for any amount of worldly treasure.

Be transformed. Be renewed. Guard your mind by filling it with the truth of God instead of the garbage of this world.

Consider:

What do you fill your head with all week? Think about the TV shows you watch, movies you've seen recently, books you've read, or games you've played. What are the messages being promoted by those things? What is considered "good" or "normal" in those things? What, if anything, do they say about God or Christians?

Look up the Ten Commandments in Exodus 20:1-17. To what extent does the society you live in obey those commandments? In what ways are those commandments disobeyed? Do you think there is pressure on you, as a Christian, to disobey God's commandments or to treat lightly the things he values? *Like Sex, Lust, horrible Dress attire, Little presence in Church, Even Church leaders with*

Look up: *porn Examples, Stealing, Cheating, Lies*

Look up and write out following verses to help keep your mind on the things

of God.

1787

Ephesians 4:22–24: *That you should put away the old self and your former way of life corrupted from deceptive desires and be Renewed in the spirit of your minds and put in the New self created in Gods way for righteousness and holiness of truth*

Colossians 2:8: *(160 k) See That no one captivates you c Empty seductive things of the world*

1807

Colossians 3:1–2: _If you have raised to Christ think of what is above where Christ is seated at the right hand of God. Think of what is above and not of what is on earth_

Philippians 4:8–9: _Pg 1798   Whatever is pure, honorable lovely gracious of excellence, praise_

Humble RAP

Apply:

Pay attention this week to the subtle messages Satan is trying to sell. Think about the values being sold by the TV shows you watch, the music you listen to, and the people you associate with. Then make a commitment to stop filling your head with Satan's lies and start filling it with things which are pleasing to God. Write down two or three things you want to change about how you fill your mind and keep track of how well you keep that commitment.

I will stop: _____

_____

_____

_____

I will start: _____

_____

_____

_____

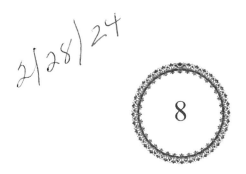

2/28/24

8

THE SWORD OF THE SPIRIT

I love a good story. I don't care if it's from a book or a movie or if someone is just sitting around spinning a tale. I like romantic stories, funny stories, mysteries, and real-life adventures. But I have always had a special place in my heart for fantasy. Even as an adult, I still love reading fairy tales, and I'm a big fan of *The Chronicles of Narnia* series and *The Lord of the Rings* trilogy.

I love the make-believe lands and interesting characters in fantasy stories, but most of all I love the battles. Some battles are big with many lives at stake, like the Battle of the Five Armies in *The Hobbit*. Others are personal, with two men facing each other alone with drawn swords, like Inigo Montoya and Count Rugen in *The Princess Bride*.

If you've ever been to a Renaissance festival or a comic convention, you've probably seen real swords and other ancient weapons for sale. At Disneyland, you can buy toy replicas of pirate daggers, Aladdin's scimitar, King Arthur's Excalibur, and futuristic lightsabers.

Children often take up a stick or broom handle to duel to the death with some imaginary enemy. I've seen plenty of adults do it, too. Having a good weapon in our hands makes us feel brave and invincible—even if our "enemy" is just a tree or a couch cushion.

In Bible times, Roman soldiers carried a sword which was very real and very deadly. A Roman sword was about eighteen inches long and sharpened on both sides. It was designed for close combat against a single opponent. A soldier needed to know how to wield the sword with accuracy and strength to block the thrusts of his enemy and to drive his own sword in for the kill. Regular training, practice, and exercise were needed to keep a soldier in top condition—anything less might cost him his life in battle.

In his letter to the Ephesians, Paul used the armor of a Roman soldier to explain how a Christian can be protected from attacks from our enemy, Satan:

> ➤ We need to have truth wrapped tightly around us to keep Satan's lies from tripping us up.
> ➤ We need to live with righteousness to keep Satan from taking away our eternal reward, our life's purpose, our relationship with God, and our good witness.
> ➤ We need to remember the gospel of peace and stand confident in the knowledge that God will provide all we need.
> ➤ We need to fully rely on God, growing in our faith as we find him faithful.
> ➤ And we need to find daily salvation for our minds by focusing on the things God values instead of Satan's garbage.

Of course, a soldier's life involves more than just being protected. A Roman soldier had to know how to fight to drive the enemy back and win battles. We must be prepared to fight as well. So, in addition to our defensive armor, Paul told us to take up a weapon: *"the sword of the Spirit, which is the Word of God"* (Ephesians 6:17).

> ? Why do you think the Bible is called "the Word of God"?
> Do you think you can be an effective Christian without
> reading and studying the Bible? NO.

Because it is the recipe to live our lives. The way God communicates c man to draw us back to the Kingdom

The Word of God

The most famous example of someone fighting a battle with the Word of God is the story of Jesus being tempted by Satan in the wilderness:

After fasting forty days and forty nights, [Jesus] was hungry. The tempter came to him and said, "If you are the Son of God, tell these stones to become bread." Jesus answered, "It is written: 'Man does not live on bread alone, but on every word that comes from the mouth of God.'"

Matthew 4:4
Deuter - 8:3

Then the devil took him to the holy city and had him stand on the highest point of the temple. "If you are the Son of God," he said, "throw yourself down. For it is written: 'He will command his angels concerning you, and they will lift you up in their hands, so that you will not strike your foot against a stone.'" Jesus answered him, "It is also written: 'Do not put the Lord your God to the test.'"

Again, the devil took him to a very high mountain and showed him all the kingdoms of the world and their splendor. "All this I will give you," he said, "if you will bow down and worship me." Jesus said to him, "Away from me, Satan! For it is written: 'Worship the Lord your God, and serve him only.'" Then the devil left him, and angels came and attended him. (Matthew 4:2–11)

Jesus used God's Word as a sword to drive Satan away from him. He quoted Deuteronomy 8:3, 6:16, and 6:13. But did you notice? Satan quoted scripture, too—Psalm 91:11-12.

That's the way it usually goes in a duel. Both sides are armed, but only one side has the skill, training, and determination to win the battle.

The Word of God—the Bible—is many things. It is an instruction manual on how to live a life pleasing to God. It is a light in our dark times and a guide which leads us in the right direction. It contains songs of praise and words of comfort. It is God's personal, loving, purposeful communication with his children and with all who seek to know him. But it is more than that.

*By **the word of the Lord** were the heavens made, their starry host by the breath of his mouth.* (Psalm 33:6)

*Then they cried to the Lord in their trouble, and he saved them from their distress. He sent forth **his word** and healed them; he rescued them from the grave.* (Psalm 107:19–20)

*The grass withers and the flowers fall, but **the word of our God** stands forever*. (Isaiah 40:8)

*"Is not **my word** like fire," declares the Lord, "and like a hammer that breaks a rock in pieces?"* (Jeremiah 23:29)

*The **word of God** is living and active. Sharper than any double-edged sword, it penetrates even to dividing soul and spirit, joints and marrow; it judges the thoughts and attitudes of the heart.* (Hebrews 4:12)

word of God is power

> ? When is the last time you thought of your Bible as a "living and active" thing? How often do you feel the power of God's Word penetrating into your soul and spirit, cutting away at ungodly thoughts and attitudes or strengthening your faith? Have you *ever* felt that power?

God is Almighty – his words give us a plan for Peace + love

Satan's War Strategy

It's interesting that Jesus quoted from Deuteronomy in his duel with Satan in the wilderness. Deuteronomy is the book of the law given by God through Moses to the children of Israel. The law was given (Deuteronomy 1:3), spoken aloud (Deuteronomy 4:1–26:19), written out (Deuteronomy 27:2-8; 31:24), and the people were instructed to take an oath to obey all the words of the law (Deuteronomy 29:9-15).

Biblical Instruction Before Leaving Earth

It wasn't long, though, before the people broke God's law and suffered the consequences of their disobedience. Satan was active even then in turning the thoughts and hearts of the people away from the words of God.

We see Satan at work again in New Testament times, sending false teachers into the churches to confuse people about what God had to say. The writers of the New Testament spent a great deal of time refuting the lies and accusations of certain men:

> *For such men are false apostles, deceitful workmen, masquerading as apostles of Christ. And no wonder, for Satan himself masquerades as an angel of light. It is not surprising, then, if his servants masquerade as servants of righteousness. Their end will be what their actions deserve.* (2 Corinthians 11:13-15)

> *This matter arose because some false brothers had infiltrated our ranks to spy on the freedom we have in Christ Jesus and to make us slaves. We did not give in to them for a moment, so that the truth of the gospel might remain with you.* (Galatians 2:4-5)

> *But there were also false prophets among the people, just as there will be false teachers among you. They will secretly introduce destructive heresies, even denying the sovereign Lord who bought them.... Many will follow their shameful ways and bring the way of truth into disrepute. In their greed these teachers will exploit you with stories they have made up.* (2 Peter 2:1-3)

and/but

When Satan deceives us about the Word of God—when we doubt its truth, add to it instructions, take away from its commands, or twist its words to our own liking—it's as if the enemy is knocking our swords right out of our hands. We may still have our defensive armor on, but we're powerless to send Satan away from us or to break his hold on our lives.

Without the sword of the Spirit, we become like "slaves" in Satan's dungeons (Galatians 2:4). But **God's Word promises us freedom if we learn to use it and wield it with power**.

Satan works hard to deceive us—not only about the words of the Bible—but also about the power of those words. There are many people who believe in the Bible. They read it and study it, they apply it's teachings to their lives, they may even memorize it, but they have never experienced its power.

In Ephesians 6:17, Paul says to take *"the sword of the Spirit, which is the word of God."* The phrase *"sword of the Spirit"* in the original Greek literally means the Spirit's sword. The words imply possession and ownership. In other words, it's not your sword being used in your power. It is the weapon of the Holy Spirit that he uses in and through us—*in us* to cut away ungodly thoughts and attitudes in our own lives, and *through us* to reach the hearts and lives of other people where Satan is also fighting for control.

The Sword of the Spirit

Another fantasy story I enjoy is the *Harry Potter* book series. Although some Christians have stayed away from reading these books or watching the movies, I have found in them some interesting parallels to the Christian life. The fictional Harry Potter lives in two worlds—a "muggle" world and a magical one. The muggle world is mostly unaware of the existence of the magical world, so young wizards like Harry must attend special schools to learn how to use their gifts, to live productive lives, and to defend themselves against their enemies.

We also live in two worlds—a natural world and a spiritual world. Only true Christians are able to operate effectively in both worlds because the Spirit of God lives within us. No matter how much time we spend serving God in the natural world, studying our Bibles, and making godly choices, we will never learn to be effective soldiers in God's army until we recognize the spiritual side of our lives.

God is supernatural—"above or beyond what is natural; unexplainable by natural law or phenomena" (Dictionary.com). God's Word is also supernatural—it is the weapon with which the Spirit of God changes our lives, sends Satan fleeing, and opens our eyes to the wonders of a life lived in the presence of God.

To some new Christians, their first introduction into the family of God is amazing and wonderful. They devour large portions of the Bible to learn about this new world they have entered—a world where God really exists, where faith moves mountains, and where lives are changed for the better. In time, many will become accustomed to being a child of God and living within his grace, and they may forget the radical change which occurred in their lives when they first accepted Jesus' invitation to follow him.

Other Christians came to know God in a less dramatic way. Their parents or other family members may have been Christians. They may have learned about Christianity from going to church or Sunday school. For these people, making the switch from Satan's side of the battle to God's side may not have seemed like a big deal. Their lives didn't change very much when they accepted God's gift of grace and joined his family. They're looking forward to heaven as a wonderful, peaceful place where they can walk in the presence of God, but here on earth, they're just passing the time.

Don't be fooled!

This kind of powerless, disinterested living is just as much a result of Satan's work as giving in to temptation and living a life of sin! Satan doesn't want the Holy Spirit to be alive and active in your life, and he is doing all he can to keep you from giving the Spirit an opportunity to really fight.

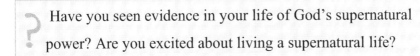

> Have you seen evidence in your life of God's supernatural power? Are you excited about living a supernatural life?

*miracles
2 near Death
Experiences*

Before Jesus left the earth, he spoke words of comfort to his disciples:

> *I will ask the Father, and he will give you another Counselor to be with you forever—the Spirit of truth. The world cannot accept him, because it neither sees him nor knows him. But you know him, for he lives with you and will be in you.* (John 14:16–17)

conscious

> *But the Counselor, the Holy Spirit, whom the Father will send in my name, will teach you all things and will remind you of everything I have said to you.* (John 14:26)

referring to the new testament

A time is coming and has now come when the true worshipers will worship the Father in spirit and truth, for they are the kind of worshipers the Father seeks. (John 4:23)

The Spirit gives life; the flesh counts for nothing. The words I have spoken to you are spirit and they are life. (John 6:63)

A Final Word

I know many Christians today are worried about the increase of books, movies, television shows, and games about supernatural and unnatural things. These shows, books, and games dealing with the supernatural are weapons Satan is using in our world today. They tempt some people to look for spiritual power not from God but from Satan. They convince others to pass off the supernatural as a hoax and a swindle, including the miraculous God of the Bible.

These same books, shows, and games present a danger to Christians as well. In our worthy efforts to flee from Satan and from his lies and temptations, we may make the mistake of distancing ourselves from anything we can't explain or understand.

Satan has fooled a lot of sincere-looking people into making false prophecies, so we might think we shouldn't believe in prophecy at all in our times. The ecstatic worship within some churches, speaking in tongues and being carried away by the spirit, can be looked on with skepticism by outsiders, so we might exercise such control when we sing and pray that we miss the supernatural stirrings of the Holy Spirit. We become so worried about how things appear in the physical world that we forget to look for what the Holy Spirit is doing in the spiritual world.

When is the last time you let the Spirit speak to your heart through the words of your Bible? When did you last hear his voice in the words of a praise song, the beauty of the melody, or the unity of the people singing around you? When is the last time you opened your eyes to the spiritual world you live in—the place where both God and Satan dwell—and seen it for what it really is?

Consider:

It's amazing how many battles occur inside church walls over the style of music played, the order of events in the service, even the color of the walls and the carpeting. Are you aware of any battles or disagreements in your church? Are these battles over things which are really important, or are they are just another way Satan is distracting people from worshipping God and learning from his Word?

Do you ever feel as if you live in two worlds? Some Christians find it hard to have faith in a supernatural God in our scientific modern world. Others accept the claims of anything asserting supernatural power, such as horoscopes, healing crystals, and eastern meditation. Where do you fall along the line between too much faith and too little? Do you scoff at some supernatural claims that could be real—or do you accept as true some claims that might be false without giving them serious consideration?

Look up:

Read through the entire 8th chapter of Romans. Make a note of how many times the word "spirit" is used: _____. Write out the promises in the verses below. Then take a good look at your life and ask yourself if you are living like a conqueror. If not, maybe it's time to let go of some of the tight control you have on your life and let the Spirit of God and his Word lead you to victory.

Romans 8:35 and 37-39: _____

_____

_____

_____

_____

_____

_____

_____

_____

_____

Apply:

A good swordsman is going to practice using his weapon every day. Make a commitment this week to read the Bible every day. Begin with a prayer that God will reveal his truths to you through his Word. Allow what you read to penetrate your life like a sharp sword as the Holy Spirit judges the thoughts and attitudes of your heart (Hebrews 4:12).

9

ALL KINDS OF PRAYERS

In the Imperial War Museum in London, England, there is a small machine that looks like an old typewriter with a number of interchangeable gears. It's an Enigma machine, used by the Germans during World War II to encrypt secret messages. The messages were relayed by radio or written communication to field commanders, undercover operatives, naval ships, and submarines, providing them with orders and crucial information about the enemy.

At an unassuming estate in the middle of England, a group of up to 9,000 code-breakers worked secretly for the British government throughout the war to decipher the codes created by the Enigma machine. The information intercepted and decoded at Bletchly Park resulted in a number of defeats for the Germans and shortened the length of the war by as much as two years.

The code-breaking operation was considered to be so important that when the unit asked for additional resources in 1941, England's Prime Minister, Winston Churchill, responded, "Make sure they have all they want on extreme priority and report to me that this had been done."

As one general put it, "The knowledge not only of the enemy's precise strength and disposition, but also how, when, and where he intends to carry out his operations brought a new dimension to the prosecution of the war."

In the Pacific, American forces were using another code—one that was never broken. Members of the Navajo tribe used words from their native language to communicate with one another by radio or telephone and then translate the message back into English. A Navajo code talker could encode, transmit, and decode a message in a small fraction of the time it took to use an encryption machine such as the Enigma. Hundreds of Navajo soldiers served with the Marines from 1942 to 1945 and are credited with saving many lives and shortening the war in the Pacific.

Since ancient times, military forces have used various means of communication to control their troops and obtain information about their opponents. Communication methods have developed considerably over the centuries to the point that information technologies have become as important to warfare as the weapons the soldiers use. In fact, many new weapons, such as unmanned aerial vehicles and laser-guided missiles would be useless without high-tech communications.

Communication is just as important in our spiritual battles. At the end of the armor of God passage in Ephesians 6, Paul tells his readers what to do once they have put on the belt of truth, the breastplate of righteousness, and shoes fitted with the gospel of peace, and taken up the shield of faith, the helmet of salvation, and the sword of the Spirit:

Pray in the Spirit on all occasions with all kinds of prayers and requests. With this in mind, be alert and always keep on praying for all the saints.

Pray also for me, that whenever I open my mouth, words may be given me so that I will fearlessly make known the mystery of the gospel, for which I am an ambassador in chains. Pray that I may declare it fearlessly, as I should. (Ephesians 6:18–20)

> **?** Who is Paul talking about when he says to pray "for all the saints"? Look up Ephesians 6:18 in different versions of the Bible to see what words they use for "saints."

What is Prayer?

I must admit that prayer has always been a mystery to me. I was taught to pray as a child when we thanked God for our food and prayed together at church. As a teenager, I brought my tearful requests to God, hoping he would take everything bad in my life and make it good. My prayers were erratic, self-centered, and, it seemed, rarely answered.

I have often heard it said that God always answers our prayers; sometimes he answers yes, sometimes he answers no, and sometimes he tells us to wait. I had trouble waiting, and I had trouble understanding all the times the answer seemed to be no. Many times, I wondered if God was listening to me at all and whether he would ever answer me clearly.

Over the years, I learned more about prayer, but I am still no expert. The exciting thing is, no one needs to be an expert to pray. All of God's children are commanded to pray, and all of God's children are heard when they pray. God wouldn't be a loving Father if he didn't listen to us when we talk to him (Matthew 7:7–11).

But the mystery remains: what is prayer? What happens when we pray? And why does Paul mention prayer at the end of the spiritual armor all God's soldiers need to use?

To begin with, it's important to understand what prayer is not.

Prayer is not a way to control God. That should be obvious, but it's amazing how many Christians lay out their prayer requests like a "Honey-do" list for God: *"God, take care of my needs." "God, keep my family safe." "God, I want that promotion at work."* God is not a vending machine, a servant, or a big Santa Claus in the sky. When we pray to God, only telling him what he needs to do for us, I'm sure he hears us, but then he frowns and turns away.

Neither should we use prayer to manipulate God. In ancient times, many cultures gave sacrifices to their gods in hopes of appeasing them and pleasing them. Their intention was to avoid disasters brought on by the gods and obtain their blessings instead. How many prayers in this country are used today to appease the one true God? The Old Testament promise, "if my people, who are called by my name, will humble themselves and pray..." (2 Chronicles 7:14), is often used as a mantra to deflect God's anger and secure his blessings.

God is not fooled by empty words of humility and repentance when the motive behind those words is our own selfish gain.

Prayer is, to put it simply, communicating with God. Communication that goes only one way is ineffectual. Communication that goes two ways—consistently, respectfully, and lovingly—accomplishes much.

But communicating with God is a little more difficult than communicating with family or friends. We pray with human words, whether we pray out loud or in our thoughts, but God rarely responds directly in human speech. So we need to learn how to listen to God in the way he speaks.

In the Bible, we see instances when God spoke directly to prophets in dreams or visions or even out of a burning bush and they recorded those words in the Bible. Today, God continues to use the Bible as one of his primary means of communication. The Holy Spirit uses the words of the Bible to speak to us individually when we read it or think on its words with an open and listening heart.

God speaks to us in other ways as well—through music, the smile of a loved one, an unexpected blessing, or the beauty of nature. Anything that lifts our thoughts to God can be used by God to communicate to us his love, his encouragement, and his guidance. If we listen for God's voice in these things, we learn to understand the language he uses, just as an infant learns to understand the language his parents use to speak to him or her every day.

 Can you think of a time you felt God communicating with you through something you read in the Bible? What about through music or the beauty of nature?

When we pray, we speak to God, but then we must listen for his answer.

I have been married for many years now. During those years, I've learned a lot about communication. I don't always understand what my husband is trying to say, so it's a good idea for me to ask questions or repeat back what I think he said. If I'm not paying attention, I'm not likely to fully understand his meaning.

Sometimes I talk and he listens without saying much of anything. If I give him the opportunity to disagree with me or to give a different viewpoint, and he doesn't take it, I can assume he's okay with whatever I've suggested; unless, of course, his body language says otherwise.

Sometimes I don't come right out and tell my husband about my wants and wishes. I want him to know me and love me enough to figure out what pleases me without a specific request. That means more to me than all the "Yes, dears" he could ever say.

Communicating with God isn't all that different.

The more we read his Word and listen for his voice, the more we understand his language. When we ask his opinion on something—Is this a good job to take? Should I marry this person? How can I manage all I have to do? —he might provide a direct answer, he might just listen and nod in agreement, or he might wait silently for us to do what we already know is pleasing to him.

As you grow in your relationship with God, you learn to understand him better, but you can't learn to understand someone if you don't take the time to communicate with that person—actively, repeatedly, and respectfully.

Our Greatest Weapon

As the Word of God is the Spirit's great weapon, prayer is ours. Through prayer, we communicate with God, telling him our problems so we can get his eternal perspective, asking him for guidance like a soldier getting his orders, and growing in our relationship with God so we find ourselves walking ever closer with him and naturally doing the things which please him.

Remember, the objective of Satan in our battles with him is twofold: to keep us from enjoying our relationship with God and to keep us from living a life that brings God glory. When we *"pray in the Spirit on all occasions with all kinds of prayers and requests"* (Ephesians 6:18) we are building up our relationship with God and preparing our hearts to serve him and bring him glory.

Satan loses. We win!

So why does prayer seem futile to so many people? Why do they feel God is not listening to them when they pray? Perhaps it's because those people have not taken the time to put on the armor of God.

The first rule for any soldier is to understand the chain of command. If you use prayer to order God around or try to manipulate him, don't be surprised if your prayers go unanswered. God is the commander in chief of this army; we are the foot soldiers.

Once you understand that, it's time to check your protective armor:

> ➢ Are you holding to the **truth** of who God is instead of letting Satan twist your image of God to fit your own liking?

> ➢ Are you being **righteous** in your daily life, doing your best to follow God's commands and trusting him to meet your needs?

> ➢ Are you standing on the **gospel of peace**, reminding yourself daily what God has done for you?

> ➢ Are you putting your **faith** in God, again and again, and seeing it grow stronger as you find God faithful?

> ➢ Are you guarding your mind by focusing on the things of God, allowing him to bring **salvation** not only for your eternal soul but for the battles of this life as well?

> ➢ Are you reading your Bible and letting the Holy Spirit speak to you, cutting into your very heart to remove what is selfish and worldly and without value to a soldier of God?

Fully suited up in our spiritual armor, we can talk to God and know we are heard. We have the assurance that he will answer, although the answer may not always be what we hope for. We also know, whatever the answer is, it will be for our good. It will be a gift from our loving heavenly Father. It will be the very thing we need to fight the battles we need to fight.

Tangle wood

So do not worry, saying, "What shall we eat?" or "What shall we drink?" or "What shall we wear?" For the pagans run after all these things, and your heavenly Father knows that you need them. But seek first his kingdom and his righteousness, and all these things will be given to you as well. (Matthew 6:31–33)

If you, then, though you are evil, know how to give good gifts to your children, how much more will your Father in heaven give good gifts to those who ask him! (Matthew 7:11)

And we know that in all things God works for the good of those who love him, who have been called according to his purpose. (Romans 8:28)

Let us then approach the throne of grace with confidence, so that we may receive mercy and find grace to help us in our time of need. (Hebrews 4:16)

> Have you been discouraged over an "unanswered" prayer? Think of that prayer specifically as you read over these verses again. Can you trust God to answer in his own time and in his own way?

The Lord's Prayer in Matthew 6:9-13 exemplifies what we should seek to accomplish through our prayers:

We begin by acknowledging God's authority over us as the Commander in Chief:

Our Father in heaven, hallowed be your name

We get our orders for the battle ahead:

your kingdom come, your will be done on earth

as it is in heaven

We make sure we have supplies:

give us today our daily bread

We get rid of unnecessary baggage:

forgive us our debts, as we also have forgiven our debtors

And we suit up in our protective armor:

and lead us not into temptation, but deliver us

from the evil one.

After that, we're ready to face the enemy and send him fleeing from us, we're set to do whatever God has called us to do that day to bring him glory, and we are actively accomplishing our mission in this world. We're **standing firm!**

A Final Word

In many respects, prayer still remains a mystery to me.

The way we pray doesn't seem to matter very much. Jesus, the apostles, and Old Testament prayer warriors prayed standing, sitting, or kneeling; alone or with other believers; out loud or silently; for their own needs and for the needs of others; but always with an emphasis on aligning their will to the will of the Father.

Paul commanded all believers to pray faithfully (Romans 12:12), with thanksgiving (Philippians 4:6), and with a vigilant attitude (Ephesians 6:18 and Colossians 4:2). Jesus spoke against those who prayed in arrogance (Luke 18:9–14) and those who babbled on in vain repetitions of the same words (Matthew 6:7). He spoke highly of those who were humble before God (Luke 18:13-14), persistent in their prayers (Luke 18:1–8), and watchful (Matthew 26:41).

Paul reminds us that prayer—like the Word of God—has much to do with the supernatural. In the Ephesians passage, Paul tells us to *"pray in the Spirit"* (Ephesians 6:18), and in Romans he states:

> *In the same way, the Spirit helps us in our weakness. We do not know what we ought to pray for, but the Spirit himself intercedes for us with groans that words cannot express. And he who searches our hearts knows the mind of the Spirit, because the Spirit intercedes for the saints in accordance with God's will.* (Romans 8:26–27)

We are also told to pray for other believers (Ephesians 6:18), which means our prayers do more than build up our own relationship with God. Our prayers affect other people, strengthening them in their battles against the enemy, too, even if they aren't aware of those prayers.

Jesus prayed for his disciples (Luke 22:31–32; John 17:6–19), for all those who would follow him (John 17:20–26), and even for those who crucified him (Luke 23:34). In the book of Hebrews we see Jesus sitting at the right hand of God, still interceding for us as a great high priest (Hebrews 4:14–16; 10:21–22). Obviously, prayer involves much more than just communicating with God about our personal needs.

In the Book of Acts, prayer is an integral ingredient of the growth of the new Church. In Acts 2:42, we see believers devoted to prayer. God responds to prayers of praise and thanksgiving in Acts 4:23–31 by shaking the room where believers are meeting. Stephen prayed while he was being stoned to death for preaching the gospel (Acts 7:59–60). The apostles prayed for Samaritan believers to receive the Holy Spirit (Acts 8:14–15). Peter prayed for life to return to a little girl (Acts 9:40). He was in prayer again when God spoke to him in a vision to accept Gentile believers into the Church (Acts 10:9–15). When Peter was miraculously released from prison by an angel, he returned to his fellow believers and found them praying (Acts 12:5–12).

Prayer runs throughout the whole Book of Acts, showing us that whenever believers sincerely called out to God, the Spirit of God was there fighting on their behalf. It could be said that prayer was the water without which the new Church could not have lived and grown.

In this day and in our churches, prayer is just as necessary for our spiritual lives and the growth of our ministries.

> **Be assured that God is listening.**
>
> **Jesus is interceding for you.**
>
> **The Holy Spirit is ready to fight on your behalf.**
>
> **All you have to do is pray.**

Consider:

Think about your prayer life over the past weeks. Are you praying "on all occasions, with all kinds of prayers and requests...for all the saints" (Ephesians 6:18)? Are you listening for God's answer, staying alert to hear his words, however he may communicate them? Are you standing firm in your faith, using your prayers to keep your guard up against Satan and his attacks?

Does your church have a special prayer time or prayer ministry? Look up Matthew 18:19-20, and consider what you could accomplish if you prayed together with fellow Christians in your Bible study, church, family, or community.

Look Up:

Write out the following verses. If you haven't already done so, commit them to memory. God is ready to do some unbelievable things in your life, your church, and your world. He's just waiting for you to ask.

Matthew 6:9-13: _____

_____

_____

_____

_____

_____

_____

Matthew 7:7–8: _____

_____

_____

_____

_____

Apply:

At the end of Chapter One, I encouraged you to pray for a persecuted Christian or group. At the end of Chapter Six, I asked you to list seven Christians you know and pray for them during the following week. Are you still praying for these people? Paul told us to *"always keep on praying for all the saints"* (Ephesians 6:18).

There is no magic formula or necessary format to follow. Keep a prayer journal, participate in an email prayer chain for your church or group, find a list of missionaries and pray for one each day. Do whatever works for you. Just pray!

God is listening, and he will answer—in his own time and in his own way. But if we really trust him, we wouldn't want it any other way!

10

THE FINAL BATTLE

On January 7, 1956, a group of missionaries flew into a remote area of Ecuador, hoping to make contact with an indigenous tribe. The five men, Jim Elliot, Pete Fleming, Ed McCully, Nate Saint, and Roger Youderian, made what seemed to be friendly contact with some of the tribesmen, although they could not understand one another's languages. However, the following day, a group from the tribe came and murdered the unsuspecting missionaries. Their story received international attention at the time and was later immortalized by a number of books and movies, including *The End of the Spear* and *Beyond the Gates of Splendor*.

These men were willing to risk their lives to take the gospel of Jesus Christ to those who had never heard it. As they said, "They're not ready for heaven—and we are." They risked everything, and gave everything, in the final battle they fought for God.

These five men were not the first to die for their faith, nor were they the last.

- ➤ Of the original twelve disciples of Jesus, it is recorded that ten died for their faith.

- ➤ The apostle Paul, who fought to the last with his spiritual armor on, was executed in Rome at the order of Emperor Nero.

- ➤ Over 20,000 Christians were martyred during the next few centuries as the Roman Empire tried to stamp out the growing Church.

- ➤ To the east of Rome, more than a thousand were killed in Persia during the same time period.

- ➤ Hundreds of thousands of Christians were killed throughout the Middle Ages and the Reformation in battles between factions of the Church, such as Roman Catholics, Eastern Orthodox, and Protestants.

- ➤ More than two million Christians were killed in 1915 after the fall of the Ottoman Empire in the Middle East.

- ➤ Some twenty million Christians were killed, tortured, or imprisoned in the early years of the Communist regime in Russia.

- ➤ Attacks on Christians in India, led by militant Hindus, resulted in a number of deaths and the displacement of 70,000 believers in the fall of 2008.

- ➤ More recently, Islamic extremists, including ISIS, Al Qaeda, and Boko Haram have murdered hundreds, if not thousands, of Christians throughout the Middle East and Africa.

The persecution of Christians has been taking place for two thousand years all around the world. It is not a political or cultural phenomenon which can be remedied with talks, protests, embargoes, or even military response. It is part of the spiritual battle between Satan and the Church.

When Jesus said, *"If they persecuted me, they will persecute you also"* (John 15:20), he was talking about all of us in the Church—past and present. But unlike the enemies who persecute us on this earth, we have God's promise of salvation and eternal life. We also have another promise from our loving Father—his judgment and vengeance:

> *When he opened the fifth seal, I saw under the altar the souls of those who had been slain because of the word of God and the testimony they had maintained. They called out in a loud voice, "How long, Sovereign Lord, holy and true, until you judge the inhabitants of the earth and avenge our blood?" Then each of them was given a white robe, and they were told to wait a little longer, until the number of their fellow servants and brothers who were to be killed as they had been was completed.*
>
> (Revelation 6:9–11)

The idea of persecution can be very scary,
especially for those who thought it couldn't happen to them.
Take a moment to pray for God to calm your fears
and to open your heart to hear his message.

The Time is Short

In 1 Corinthians, Paul addresses a number of issues of Christian living. Most of his advice involves how we live our daily lives, but his focus was the eternal impact of our lives. Paul was motivated by a sense of urgency, wanting as much as possible to be done for the gospel of Christ while there was still time:

> *What I mean, brothers, is that the time is short. From now on those who have wives should live as if they had none; those who mourn, as if they did not; those who are happy, as if they were not; those who buy something, as if it were not theirs to keep; those who use the things of the world, as if not engrossed in them. For this world in its present form is passing away.* (1 Corinthians 7:29–31)

Paul knew his own time was running out. In the next twelve years, he would be imprisoned twice for preaching the gospel. The second time, he would be sentenced to death. During his last imprisonment, he wrote to his close friend Timothy from his jail cell:

> *I am already being poured out like a drink offering, and the time has come for my departure. I have fought the good fight, I have finished the race, I have kept the faith. Now there is in store for me the crown of righteousness, which the Lord, the righteous Judge, will award to me on that day—and not only to me, but to all who have longed for his appearing.* (2 Timothy 4:6–8)

Paul was convinced that *"to die is gain,"* and he longed *"to depart and be with Christ"* (Philippians 1:21, 23), but he had no intention of leaving this life as a casualty of war. Dying for the gospel was not defeat in Paul's eyes; to the contrary, to die was gain! The greatest defeat was living a life that accomplished nothing for God's glory.

The casualties of our war against Satan are not those who die in the name of Jesus but those who never learn to live in his name.

Ironically, we live for Jesus most effectively when we focus less on our lives on earth and more on our future in heaven. It is when we look forward to the glories of meeting God and Jesus face-to-face, of walking heaven's streets of gold, and of no longer living in a cursed and dying world, that we realize how short our time is here on earth and how much we still have to accomplish.

In his last letter, Paul encouraged Timothy to continue the work Paul had begun with the same urgency:

> *In the presence of God and of Christ Jesus, who will judge the living and the dead, and in view of his appearing and his kingdom, I give you this charge: Preach the Word; be prepared in season and out of season; correct, rebuke and encourage—with great patience and careful instruction.*
>
> *For the time will come when men will not put up with sound doctrine. Instead, to suit their own desires, they will gather around them a great number of teachers to say what their itching ears want to hear. They will turn their ears away from the truth and*

To days
DEMS

131

turn aside to myths. But you, keep your head in all situations, endure hardship, do the work of an evangelist, discharge all the duties of your ministry. (2 Timothy 4:1–5)

Paul wrote more than once about the return of Jesus Christ, and he may have believed it would not be long in coming. But two thousand years later, we are left with Paul's admonition to use our time wisely, to stand firm in our faith—even to the point of death—and to look forward with great expectation to Christ's glorious return:

Listen, I tell you a mystery: We will not all sleep, but we will all be changed—in a flash, in the twinkling of an eye, at the last trumpet. For the trumpet will sound, the dead will be raised imperishable, and we will be changed. For the perishable must clothe itself with the imperishable, and the mortal with immortality. When the perishable has been clothed with the imperishable, and the mortal with immortality, then the saying that is written will come true: "Death has been swallowed up in victory."

Where, O death, is your victory? Where, O death, is your sting? The sting of death is sin, and the power of sin is the law. But thanks be to God! He gives us the victory through our Lord Jesus Christ.

Therefore, my dear brothers, stand firm. Let nothing move you. Always give yourselves fully to the work of the Lord, because you know that your labor in the Lord is not in vain. (1 Corinthians 15:51–58)

> **?**
> What would you do differently in your daily life if you
> believed your time on earth would be cut short?
> Are you anxiously waiting for Jesus' return or
> are you too focused on the things of this world?

[handwritten margin notes: Pray more / Travel / Be Kinder / Less worry over Future / Less Emphasis on = Things]

The End of the Age

Although it's something many people don't like to think about, the end times—the final years leading up to Jesus' return to earth and what happens after that—are talked about repeatedly throughout the Bible. There are prophecies about the end times in the Old Testament books of Isaiah, Jeremiah, Ezekiel, Daniel, Joel, Zephaniah, and Zechariah. Jesus spoke of the "end of the age" in Matthew 24, Mark 13, and Luke 21. Paul talked about the return of Christ in 1 Corinthians 15, 1 Thessalonians 4–5, and 2 Thessalonians 2. Almost the entire book of Revelation is an outline of the earth's final years.

Jesus describes "the end of the age" in bleak terms:

You will hear of wars and rumors of wars, but see to it that you are not alarmed. Such things must happen, but the end is still to come. Nation will rise against nation, and kingdom against kingdom. There will be famines and earthquakes in various places. All these are the beginning of birth pains.

[handwritten note: Mark 13·32]

Then you will be handed over to be persecuted and put to death, and you will be hated by all nations because of me. At that time many will turn away from the faith and will betray and hate each other, and many false prophets will appear and deceive many people. Because of the increase of wickedness, the love of most will grow cold.... Then there will be great distress, unequaled from the beginning of the world until now—and never to be equaled again. If those days had not been cut short, no one would survive, but for the sake of the elect those days will be shortened. (Matthew 24:6–12, 21–22)

Revelation paints a similar picture: massive battles; famine and plagues; turmoil in the sea, sky, and land; and the persecution of those who hold to the testimony of Jesus. Paul says *"There will be terrible times in the last days"* (2 Timothy 3:1).

Why was so much information given in the Old and New Testaments about events which wouldn't happen for thousands of years? Are these warnings being given for those Christians who will be alive at the time of the end? Or are they meant to be heeded by all Christians in all times?

The answer is yes—to both questions. These warnings are given not so that we will be frightened and anxious about the future, but so that we will be prepared, spiritually and mentally, for the difficult days which may be ahead for any one of us.

Jesus told many parables about being ready (Matthew 22:2–14; 25:1–13), being watchful (Matthew 24:43; Mark 13:34–37), interpreting the times (Matthew 24:32–34; Luke 12:54–56), and making good use of our limited time (Matthew 24:45–51, 25:14–30; Luke 13:6–9). Paul spoke with great urgency about doing the work of God with a clear focus (1 Corinthians 7:29, 9:24). The writer of Hebrews also encouraged us to push forward with determination like runners racing to the finish line (Hebrews 12:1).

Our lives here on earth are like *"grass [that] withers and the flowers [that] fall"* (Isaiah 40:6–8) and like a *"mist that appears for a little while and then vanishes"* (James 4:14). If we want to be greeted in heaven with the commendation, *"Well done, good and faithful servant"* (Matthew 25:21, 23), we would do well to live our lives as if Jesus' return is going to happen any day!

But the warnings given about the last times may also be for Christians who will have to live through those years—or die during them.

The *Left Behind* series by Tim LaHaye and Jerry B. Jenkins popularized the idea that Christians will be "raptured" and taken up into the sky at the beginning of the Great Tribulation, the final seven years before Jesus returns to earth to defeat Satan and set up a one-thousand-year reign. It makes Christians feel good to think they will be pulled out of the war zone before all the terrible things the Bible talks about take place. Such a belief can also keep Christians from preparing themselves for the worst, even though each one of us could face a time of persecution and tribulation in our own lives at any time.

Some Bible scholars believe Christians will not be raptured until the end of the tribulation when Jesus returns to earth to fight the final battle. The warnings about great persecution, being hated by all nations, and being on guard against false prophets may be intended for all believers alive at the time the Antichrist comes on the scene, not just a few gentile and Jewish converts who turn to Jesus after the rapture.

In Revelation, when John sees *"the souls of those who had been beheaded because of their testimony for Jesus and because of the word of God, [who] had not worshiped the beast or his image and had not received his mark on their foreheads or their hands"* (Revelation 20:4), he could be talking about any one of us.

But remember, these are not casualties of war in the eyes of God; these are the "blessed" victors who will come alive and reign with Jesus for a thousand years (Revelation 20:4–6)!

The Book of Revelation contains seven blessings given primarily to those who will see the events of the book take place. **In the midst of the greatest distress and suffering this cursed world has ever known, God makes it clear who is winning the battle:**

> *Blessed is the one who reads the words of this prophecy, and blessed are those who hear it and take to heart what is written in it, because the time is near.* (Revelation 1:3)

> *Blessed are the dead in the Lord from now on.... They will rest from their labor, for their deeds will follow them.* (Revelation 14:13)

> *Behold, I come like a thief! Blessed is he who stays awake and keeps his clothes with him, so that he may not go naked and be shamefully exposed.* (Revelation 16:15)

> *Blessed are those who are invited to the wedding supper of the Lamb!* (Revelation 19:9)

Blessed and holy are those who have part in the first resurrection. The second death has no power over them, but they will be priests of God and of Christ and will reign with him for a thousand years. (Revelation 20:6)

Behold, I am coming soon! Blessed is he who keeps the words of the prophecy written in this book. (Revelation 22:7)

Blessed are those who wash their robes, that they may have the right to the tree of life and may go through the gates into the city. (Revelation 22:14)

A Final Word

When people enlist or are drafted into the army, they go in understanding they might at some point be involved in a real battle. They could be injured, they could be captured by the enemy, they could even be killed. That thought is driven home every time a soldier puts on his battle armor, every time he picks up a weapon, and every time he writes a letter home wondering if it will be his last. Soldiering is serious business, and it's the soldier who is fully prepared for the worst who is best able to complete the mission and live to fight another day.

We know God has promised us a lifetime of blessings, he has a plan and a purpose for our lives, and he loves us and wants the best for us, but he has also called us to be soldiers in a lifelong battle. You might think that's a raw deal. You might wonder if following God is really worth it.

It is worth it!

Satan is a liar, and he wants to trap you with his lies. God offers truth to set you free.

Do you trust him?

Satan offers a life of pleasures and acceptance in the world, but God says you can enjoy his riches and have a life of purpose only if you obey him and live a righteous life.

Do you trust him?

Satan tries to destroy your peace of mind with negative emotions and attitudes. God offers peace in the midst of trials and troubles.

Do you trust him?

Satan wants to shoot you down with fiery insults and personal attacks. God says to have faith in him and be all you were meant to be.

Do you trust him?

Satan's goal is to undermine everything that has value to God, but God offers you salvation from Satan's garbage.

Do you trust him?

Satan will do anything to twist the Word of God, to challenge it, and to weaken your hold on it, but the Holy Spirit can use this sword to bring victory to your life.

Do you trust him?

Paul said, *"Everyone who wants to live a godly life in Christ Jesus will be persecuted"* (2 Timothy 3:12), but Jesus told us, *"Blessed are you when people insult you, persecute you and falsely say all kinds of evil against you because of me. Rejoice and be glad, because great is your reward in heaven, for in the same way they persecuted the prophets who were before you"* (Matthew 5:11–12).

Do you trust him?

That's what it comes down to—do you trust him? Are you ready to put on your armor, take up your weapons, and join the fight?

The time is short. The battle is already going on. The end is certain: Satan loses, God wins. Whose side will you be on?

> May God himself, the God of peace, sanctify you through and through. May your whole spirit, soul and body be kept blameless at the coming of our Lord Jesus Christ. The one who calls you is faithful and he will do it.
>
> 1 Thessalonians 5:23–24

Look up:

Look up and read Revelation 22:1-5. Then write out Revelation 22:20:

_____

_____

_____

_____

APPENDIX

THE SOLDIER OF GOD

In the book of Ephesians, Paul told Christians to *"put on the full armor of God,"* including the belt of truth, the breastplate of righteousness, and shoes fitted with the gospel of peace, and then to *"take up"* the shield of faith, the helmet of salvation, and the sword of the Spirit (Ephesians 6:11–17). These items not only offer protection to the children of God. They also define who *is* a child of God. Just like a Roman soldier was known by his uniform, we can be certain we belong to God if we have taken up his armor.

The Helmet of Salvation: *"Salvation is found in no one else, for there is no other name under heaven given to men by which we must be saved"* (Acts 4:12). Salvation from the coming judgment of all mankind and from the penalty of our sins comes only from Jesus Christ.

The Shield of Faith: *"For it is by grace you have been saved, through faith—and this not from yourselves, it is the gift of God—not by works, so that no one can boast"* (Ephesians 2:8–9). Faith means more than just believing about God and Jesus and salvation. It means accepting that belief, making it yours, and letting it change your life.

The Breastplate of Righteousness: *"But now a righteousness from God, apart from law, has been made known, to which the Law and the Prophets testify. This righteousness from God comes through faith in Jesus Christ to all who believe"* (Romans 3:21–22). Because Jesus lived a sinless life and took the penalty for our sins on the Cross, our sins are covered by his righteousness, and we can stand in the presence of God, holy and without blame.

Feet Fitted with the Gospel of Peace: *"Therefore, since we have been justified through faith, we have peace with God through our Lord Jesus Christ"* (Romans 5:1). When we accept God's free gift of salvation through faith in Jesus' death and resurrection we change sides in the eternal battle between good and evil, God and Satan. We join God's side and live at peace with him forever.

The Belt of Truth: This is the hard one and the one that has to come first. If we try to come to God on our terms instead of accepting the truth of what he has to say in his Word, we'll find ourselves on the wrong side of the battle lines when we finally stand before our Judge.

To become a Christian by faith in Jesus Christ, we have to agree with him that we are sinners in need of a savior (Romans 3:23). We have to understand that the penalty for our sin is death (Romans 6:23). We have to accept that we cannot please God on our own because we are cursed people living in a cursed world (Romans 8:5–8). We need to confess our sins, but we also have to repent of them, to turn away from sin and turn toward our loving God (Acts 20:21). Then, and only then, will we be called the children of God. Then all his armor—salvation, faith, peace, righteousness, and truth—will be ours for all eternity.

If you have never faced the truth about God's plan of salvation, if you have never confessed your sins and accepted God's free gift of eternal life through faith in Jesus Christ, I invite you to do so now. Find someone to talk to who knows God, and read this book to help you understand God's plan for your life. Satan wants you to miss out and stay enslaved by his lies and the useless pleasures of life. Why not choose the winning side of the battle instead?

NOTES

NOTES

NOTES

NOTES

ABOUT THE AUTHOR

Janet Ruth is a wife, mother, and writer.
She holds a master's degree in Biblical Studies as well as a
law degree.
Janet combines her love of research and her years of
experience as a trial attorney and a college professor to teach
important Christian doctrines and help her readers develop a
strong Christian worldview.

Read more about Janet and her books at
www.JaneTruth.com

Made in the USA
Columbia, SC
20 June 2023

18333531R00095